# Warren Buffett

## ── SPEAKS ──

**Wit and Wisdom from the World's Greatest Investor**

# Warren Buffett

## SPEAKS

### Wit and Wisdom from the World's Greatest Investor

Completely Revised and Updated

## JANET LOWE

John Wiley & Sons, Inc.

Published by John Wiley & Sons, Inc., Hoboken, New Jersey.
Published simultaneously in Canada.

Wiley Bicentennial Logo: Richard J. Pacifico.

For general information on our other products and services or for technical
support, please contact our Customer Care Department within the United
States at (800) 762-2974, outside the United States at (317) 572-3993 or fax
(317) 572-4002.

Wiley also publishes its books in a variety of electronic formats. Some content
that appears in print may not be available in electronic formats. For more
information about Wiley products, visit our Web site at www.wiley.com.

ISBN 978-0-470-15262-1

Printed in the United States of America.

10  9  8  7  6  5  4  3  2  1

*To my patient family.*
　　　　—JCL

# Contents

# — Acknowledgments —

Many generous people helped in the preparation of this book. Thanks to Pam Buffett; Warren Buffett; Jolene Crowley; Elizabeth Douglass; *San Diego Union-Tribune;* Lorena Goeller; Arthur Q. Johnson; Steve Jorden; *Omaha World-Herald;* Irving Kahn, Kahn Brothers; Kathy Lowe; Bruce Marks; Charles T. Munger; The North Carolina Public Television Foundation and the Kenan-Flagler School of Business, University of North Carolina, Chapel Hill; Doerthe Obert; Walter Schloss of Walter & Edwin Schloss; R. Hutchings Vernon; Kathy Welton; my editor, Kevin Commins; and my literary agent, Alice Fried Martell. Also, I am grateful to have been able to talk to Susan T. Buffett, Katharine Graham, and Sequoia fund founder William Ruane before their deaths.

# Warren Buffett

## SPEAKS

### Wit and Wisdom from the World's Greatest Investor

# Introduction

Is there anyone anywhere who has more nicknames than Warren Buffett? *Vanity Fair* called him the Forrest Gump of finance.[1] He's been dubbed the Oracle of Omaha, Omaha's plain dealer, the corn-fed capitalist, St. Warren (with a less than admiring inflection), and the financial world's Will Rogers. He could also be called the king of bling for his ownership of jewelry stores, including the second-largest in the United States, Borsheim's of Omaha.

Several books attempt to capture the personality, the philosophy, and the very essence of the world's most successful investor; but words fail to adequately describe this unique individual . . . except perhaps his own words. Nobody does Warren Buffett as well as Warren Buffett. It was this realization that inspired this collection of his aphorisms and observations.

Who is this modern American hero/questionable saint? Here are the basics. The details will unfold as you read the rest of the book . . . told in his own words.

Warren Edward Buffett was born August 30, 1930, in Omaha, Nebraska. He attended grade school there but went to junior high and high school in the Washington, D.C., area, where his father, Howard Homan Buffett, served four terms in the U.S. House of Representatives. In college, Warren abandoned the Wharton School at the University of Pennsylvania because he didn't think he was learning anything. He enrolled at the University of Nebraska (Lincoln campus), where he earned a bachelor of science degree in 1950. He then applied to Harvard but was rejected. Instead, Buffett earned a master of science in economics from Columbia University in 1951. It was at Columbia that he met the great investor Professor Benjamin Graham, who soon became Buffett's mentor and friend.

Buffett and Susan Thompson, an Omaha neighbor, were married in 1952. The couple raised three children: one daughter and two sons. The Buffetts resided in separate cities for many years. They were a close and affectionate couple, but their relationship puzzled many people. Susan passed away from a stroke in 2004. (By the way, Susie with an *s* refers to Susan the mother, and Suzie with a *z* refers to Susan the daughter.)

Susan Buffett, who with her husband owned a majority interest in Berkshire Hathaway, was a vivacious, empathetic person whom Buffett described as "a free spirit." She lived in San Francisco and told me, "I have a quiet life of my own with my family and people I love." Buffett continued to live in Omaha. Several years after Susie's death, Warren remarried.

A lot has happened since I first wrote *Warren Buffett Speaks* in 1997, and yet a few things have remained the same. Let's begin with the things that are the same: Back then, Warren Buffett was the most amazing investor in the United States, and he remains a plus ultra business leader. He was among the top richest Americans then and still is number two. Berkshire Hathaway was the most unusual (and highest-priced) stock in the world, and it remains so.

Buffett continues to collect an annual salary of $100,000, making him the lowest-paid executive among the largest 200 companies in the country.

Now for the changes: As Buffett always said would happen, as Berkshire Hathaway has continued to grow in size, the difficulties of investing the mountains of cash also compound. Expansion and innovation have taken place at Berkshire as it evolves, but the most dramatic movements have been in Buffett's personal life.

While Buffett was fairly well-known when I first started writing about him, he was not instantly recognized by those who had no connection to the financial world. Buffett first stepped to center stage when he became financial adviser to California gubernatorial candidate Arnold Schwartzenegger; he came fully into the spotlight when he dedicated some $30 billion (yes, that's a *b*, not an *m*) in assets to the Bill and Melinda Gates Foundation.

In both his financial life and his civic life, noted *Vanity Fair* magazine, "his biggest job has become managing his own impact."[2] That impact could not have been more obvious than in February 2007, when shares of the New York Times Co. rose 3.8 percent in a single day on rumors that Buffett was buying shares of newspaper companies. Although Buffett has said newspapers are no longer economically interesting, the N.Y. Times Co. might have been a temptation to the value investor in him because, between 2004 and 2007, its shares had fallen 44 percent.

Some business events have been uncomplicated, such as Buffett selling his minority ownership in the Omaha Royals baseball team. Others have been significant and stressful, such as severe stock market swings and difficulties with the purchase of General Re insurance company. Perhaps the most surprising advance at Berkshire has been its foray into foreign investments.

There have been painful and significant transitions in Buffett's personal life. Some important people have passed on, including his wife, his mother, and his beloved friends Katharine Graham, Rose Blumkin, William Ruane, and Philip Carret. Susan's death led to other momentous changes in his personal life, such as the restructuring of his plans for charitable giving and the Gates Foundation contribution. And Buffett's children seem to have come more fully into their own identity. At least the world is getting to know them better. Buffett publicly recognized their autonomy and maturity by making generous contributions to their own charitable trusts. Incidentally, the contributions to the children's trusts give some idea of how talented an investor their father is. When Warren and Susie first established the children's charitable trusts, they funded the foundations with 129 shares of Berkshire class A stock and 68 shares of class B stock at a cost of just over $2,000. The present value of the stock is $11,353,806—a growth of $11,351,614.

This book looks at what makes Warren Buffett special among the world's billionaires. The former head of Coca-Cola, Don Keough, once said that Buffett's life story was not about money but about values. This remains the most constant fact about Buffett.

Buffett's professional record speaks for itself. His first investment fund, the Buffett Partnership, ran from 1956 to 1969 with a record of 32 percent average annual return before fees. Shortly after the 100-member partnership closed, Buffett began transforming Berkshire Hathaway from a textile manufacturer to a holding company/investment vehicle that has no exact parallel on Wall Street. When Buffett bought his first 200 shares of Berkshire Hathaway, the stock was selling at $7.50 per share, plus 10 cents per share commission. Buffett took control of Berkshire Hathaway in 1965, when shares were trading between $12 and $15. In its 42 years under Buffett's tutelage, Berkshire's per-share book value has grown at twice the rate of the Standard & Poor's 500 index. Dozens of people who invested with Buffett when he first started managing money remain with him today—or their heirs do.

Despite his influence and affluence, Buffett continues to be plainspoken, honest, optimistic, and funny. *The Economist* described Buffett in handling the Salomon Inc./U.S. government bond scandal as "fast, frank, and folksy";[5] and that's pretty much the way he does everything. He follows a simple wisdom; but it would be a mistake to underestimate his intelligence, knowledge, or resolve. Buffett sets very tough standards and sticks to them.

My suspicion is that Buffett purposely retains his homespun language and explains things in parable form to better communicate with us mere mortals. When he lets loose with his full vocabulary and intellect, many of us would be lost.

Though Buffett is invariably polite, he does not spend time on projects, concepts, or people unless they interest him, seem worthy, or relate to his bottom line. He can be impatient when his patience is tried. For example, though he seldom couches criticism in personal terms, Buffett has few kind words for academicians who chase one investment theory after another, failing to acknowledge the basic, underlying economic function of stocks and the stock market. He cuts no slack for advisers who lure investors into speculative ventures. Inaccurate or imprecise journalism raises his hackles.

When Buffett speaks or writes, people listen. Shareholders, family members, and friends crowd into Omaha to attend Berkshire's annual meeting and to hear him. Investors gather all over town to swap Buffett stories. Those with the earliest Berkshire Hathaway purchase dates are the elite.

In the early 1980s, shares were trading around $500; only about 15 attended the annual meeting. By the late 1980s, shares were trading around $2,500; about 400 shareholders attend the meeting. Through the 1990s, Buffett moved to progressively larger venues as attendance grew. By 2006, 10,000 Buffett fans burst the seams of Omaha's largest meeting space, the Qwest Center.

The late William Ruane, founder of Sequoia Fund, had been Buffett's friend since they met in Benjamin Graham's seminar at Columbia University. Ruane described Buffett's speaking skills this way: "Warren is a genius, but he can explain something so simply and with such clarity that, at least at that moment, you understand exactly what he is saying."

"Warren's gift is being able to think ahead of the crowd," wrote Bill Gates, chief executive of Microsoft and a Berkshire board member, "and it requires more than taking his aphorisms to heart to accomplish that—although Warren is full of aphorisms worth taking to heart."[4]

Once, Buffett's storytelling habit earned him a rap on the knuckles. He was testifying as an expert witness in a federal case, and the attorney asked him a question. "Please, Mr. Buffett," the judge interjected, "not another story." Buffett protested that this was his manner of communicating. The judge sighed, and Buffett spun his yarn.[5]

By way of disclosure, I have interviewed and met Buffett numerous times and admit to liking him. This may lead the reader to assume that I will try to present Buffett in the best light. That is not my objective. It is my goal to demonstrate his unusual way of thinking and to let the readers make their own value judgments. I've included incidents where Buffett's behavior is difficult to understand, along with points of view of those who don't think he's so terrific. Nevertheless, I admit the material is presented in a mostly friendly light. After all, if I didn't think Buffett had useful things to say, I would not have spent so much time and energy on this book. Considering the enormous pressure now put on him by a wide range of "others," he does a commendable job of being himself.

A cheerful good humor and lack of malice dominate Buffett's personality. His parents obviously told him that if he couldn't say something nice about a person, he shouldn't say anything at all; and he believed it. But there is also a subtle quality to his demeanor that implies he means what he does say. Although he is open to ideas, unless you have something new, constructive, and convincing to add to his information, he is unlikely to be swayed. Some people gain this kind of self-confidence with age; Buffett apparently has long been sure of what he thought and was ready to explain his point of view.

This compilation of Buffett's quotations could be called *A Life's Little Lesson Book* for investors. The sayings (plus anecdotes by and about Buffett) are organized under broad general categories, and beneath those categories are specific headings. The topic headings are followed by one or more quotations, a little story, or a short account of an event. When necessary, I have placed the quotation in its proper setting. Each quote is a small clue to the philosophy by which Buffett lives while creating, managing, and dispersing wealth for himself and many, many others. Included are segments about significant friends, family, colleagues, and events; what these people and incidents say about Buffett; and what the players have to say about themselves and their role in the Buffett saga.

I have tried to give the reader a sense of Buffett's personality through selection, placement, and treatment of the quotes. Even though the collection is conversational in tone, please remember that this is a collage. The comments did not necessarily occur in the order listed here, nor were comments on related topics necessarily said at the same time. To help keep track of Buffett's life, there is a time line at the end of the book.

Buffett's comments don't always translate perfectly from speech to written word, sorry to say. To a certain extent, it's Buffett's delivery that makes his comments so entertaining. Though Buffett speaks well, when he is relaxed and talking without notes—which is always—his grammar is not perfect. But whose is? He *uh*s and *um*s his way through a statement and then repeats himself. He can speak for 10 minutes without ending a sentence, each phrase connected by "and." When it seems the best way to get a point across, I've quoted the exact wording, including imperfections. When possible, I've emphasized the words he emphasized.

In an occasional rare instance, for the sake of clarity and space, I copy edited ever so slightly. *Um*s and *uh*s were eliminated, or the noun and the verb were made to match in terms of past and present, plural or singular. In almost all cases, the change is in brackets. This was done with meticulous care to preserve Buffett's intention and meaning. It is important to Buffett that he be understood clearly. I once was with him in New York. Several hours after he spoke, Buffett was handed a copy of a wire service story about his comments. There was a small but significant error in the story. "I don't think I said that. Did I say that? No, I don't think I did." He clearly was disturbed that this misquotation would be repeated worldwide; would mostly likely go into many, many research databases; and in time would be chiseled in marble.

So, whenever it appeared that a quotation was or could be misinterpreted, the discrepancy is discussed in the text.

In compiling this book, I have noticed some intriguing patterns. For example, Buffett started measuring the value of many things—the price of his wife's engagement ring, for example—in terms of net worth at an age when most people didn't know how to figure their net worth; or if they did know how, they would come up with a negative number. He also likes the "pretend you're going away for (5, 10, . . .) years" construct. He writes his annual reports to a sister who has been on an extended vacation or suggests investing as if you wouldn't be able to change your mind for a decade. "Punching tickets" and "accumulating claim checks" are common Buffett metaphors.

Readers may observe patterns that I have missed. It has been interesting to see how others interpret and what they glean from *Warren Buffett Speaks*.

Willa Cather fans will recognize immediately in Buffett the unpretentious intelligence, balance, depth, and sense of authority over oneself that the Nebraska-reared novelist saw in her fellow Plainspeople. Cather did not claim, however, that heartlanders were simple in their psychology or unflawed in their nature. This said, it is up to each of us to decide for ourselves who the real Warren Buffett is.

# —— About Life ——

When Warren Buffett speaks on stock markets, business ethics, or the price of corn in Nebraska, ears perk up all over the world. His words often have relevance beyond the immediate issue. They bring forth an "Ah ha!" or "Of course!" Buffett's comments seem to touch many aspects of our lives. Though he ranks among the wealthiest people in the world, his friend Charlie Munger says that Buffett also is one of the happiest people he knows. Before reading what Buffett has to say about successful investing, let's see what he says about the more important subjects of living productively and being content.

## OMAHA? OMAWHERE? OMAWHAT?

Warren Buffett—or "Fireball," as his dad called him—spent his early years attending public school in Omaha.

When his father, Howard Buffett, was elected to the U.S. House of Representatives, the family moved to the nation's capital. Young Warren pined to go back home:

*"I was miserably homesick. I told my parents I couldn't breathe when lying down. I told them not to worry about it, to get a good night's sleep themselves, and I'd just stand up all night."*

Eventually, 12-year-old Warren was allowed to return to Omaha to live with his grandfather until the end of the school term.[1] Clearly, Warren agreed with those who call it the "beautiful island of Omaw-hah."

Buffett later attended Wharton School of Business at the University of Pennsylvania and graduate school at Columbia University. He worked for the Graham-Newman Company in New York; but in early 1956, at age 25, he went home to Omaha to stay:

*"I've lived in New York and Washington, but the logistics of New York take a lot of time. I can get the pluses of New York and Los Angeles by getting on a plane and flying for three hours, but I pay no penalty by having to live there."* [2]

~

*"I think it's a saner existence here. I used to feel, when I worked back in New York, that there were more stimuli just hitting me all the time, and you've got the*

*normal amount of adrenaline, you start responding to them. It may lead to crazy behavior after a while. It's much easier to think here."* [3]

Buffett's younger son, Peter, a musician, composed a song called "Nebraska." It reflects a similar love of America's heartland: "It expresses how strongly I feel about having the foundation, the solidity, the spiritual roots of a homeland," Peter Buffett said of his composition.

## LIVE HOW YOU WANT TO LIVE

"One of the things that attracted me to working with securities was the fact that you could live your own life. You don't have to dress for success," said Warren Buffett. [4]

*"I can't think of anything in life I want that I don't have."* [5]

Is Buffett's lifestyle merely the path of least resistance for him?

*"It's easier to create money than to spend it."* [6]

## EAT WHAT YOU WANT TO EAT

If we are what we eat, Buffett has been all-American:

*"My ideas about food and diet were irrevocably formed quite early—the product of a wildly successful party*

*that celebrated my fifth birthday. On that occasion we had hot dogs, hamburgers, soft drinks, popcorn, and ice cream."*

Buffett's signature dish is a Dusty Sundae: He pours lots of Hershey's Chocolate Syrup over vanilla ice cream and then heaps malted milk powder over that. He justifies the calories mathematically:

*"The caloric consumption produced by this concoction is inconsequential. Assume that your basal metabolism rate is 2,800 calories per day. Simple arithmetic tells us that you can—indeed you must—consume slightly over 1 million calories per year. In my own case—with a life expectancy of about 25 years—this means that, in order to avoid premature death through starvation, I need to eat some 25 million calories. Why not get on with it?"*[7]

There are times, however, when calories aren't worth the cost. Buffett once was offered a glass of high-priced wine at a dinner party. Holding his hand over his glass, he replied:

*"No, thanks. I'll take cash."*[8]

## HAVE A HOBBY

Investing is both sport and entertainment for Buffett. He likens finding a good acquisition to "bagging rare and fast-moving elephants."[9]

However, friends, family, and the card game of bridge fill his spare time. He gathers with family and friends for special occasions, such as to celebrate an award given by the Omaha YWCA to his daughter for her work on The Rose Theater, and for Bill Gates's wedding on the Hawaiian island of Lanai.

Every other year, he organizes a meeting of the Buffett Group, a gathering of his longest and dearest friends. Although he quit racquetball after injuring his back, he still occasionally plays golf; and at the 1996 annual meeting, a noticeably slimmer Buffett explained that he'd taken up working out on a treadmill. The audience noticed that he'd also switched to sipping Diet Coke at the meeting, versus Classic or Cherry Coke.

Bridge has been Buffett's great passion; and under the guidance of an expert coach, his card game has risen to new levels. He likes the game so much that he says:

*"Any young person who doesn't take up bridge is making a big mistake."* [10]

Buffett played bridge with *Forbes* publisher Malcolm Forbes the night before the flamboyant capitalist died of a heart attack. The game took place in Forbes's London mansion, and it pitted Corporate America's Six Honchos (CASH) against British members of Parliament. The CASH team consisted of Buffett, Forbes, Bear Stearns chairman Alan "Ace" Greenberg, CBS chairman Laurence Tisch, and several other Americans. They played morning and afternoon, with the CASH team first losing to bridge-playing members of the House of Lords and then besting members of the House of Commons.

*"I don't think about anything else when I play bridge."*[11]

~

*"I always said I wouldn't mind going to jail if I had three cellmates who played bridge."*[12]

Buffett's bridge coach (Sharon Osberg is a world champion player whom he met through bridge-playing friend Carol Loomis) introduced him to the computer and to ImagiNation, a network that allows him to play cards from home with friends around the country.

*"I'd walk by a PC and be afraid it might bite me, but once I got started it was easy."*

Thanks to the computer, Buffett now cuts the deck with his sister and her husband who live in Carmel, California; distinguished friends in Washington, D.C.; and even William H. Gates Sr., the Seattle attorney whose famous son founded Microsoft Inc.:

*"Now it is much easier to get the game up and running with the same people I usually played with, only now we all sit thousands of miles apart. I played for six*

*hours one Sunday. I don't play as many face-to-face games anymore."*[13]

Bill Gates explained what followed:

*"Despite the fact that he had studiously stayed away from technology and technology investing, once he tried the computer, he was hooked. Now, many weeks, Warren uses online services more than I do."*[14]

## BE PASSIONATE

Passion sometimes involves spending money, as it did when Buffett bought his corporate jet, "The Indefensible." Buffett considered naming the plane "The Charles T. Munger" in honor of his partner, who still resolutely flew economy class:

*"I've fallen in love with the plane. It's going to be buried with me."*[15]

After Buffett went to New York for nearly a year to work through problems at Salomon Inc., he began calling his plane "The Semidefensible."[16]

But, alas, love affairs sometimes end. When Berkshire acquired NetJets Inc. in 1995, both Buffett and Munger, started using the corporate-jet, fractional-ownership service. Now Buffett sings the praises of NetJets.

Buffett has had a lifetime love for cola drinks, first Pepsi-Cola and later Coca-Cola (Cherry Coke, to be precise). The Buffetts once threw a party, and the late Susie Buffett decorated the entrance with 3-foot-tall Pepsi bottles in the front windows.

"Everybody who knows Warren knows he doesn't have a bloodstream—it's a Pepsi stream; he even has it for breakfast," Susie said.

## AIM HIGH

Now that you are the richest man in America, asked a shareholder at a Berkshire Hathaway annual meeting, what is your next goal? "That's easy," Buffett replied. "To be the oldest man in America."[17]

But he doesn't believe in overreaching:

*"I don't try to jump over seven-foot bars: I look around for one-foot bars that I can step over."*[18]

## ATTENTION INVESTORS: WARREN BUFFETT IS CROSSING THE STREET

At the 1996 annual meeting, an investor asked what would happen to Berkshire Hathaway if Buffett were to get hit by a truck. The question pops up more often than toast at breakfast. "I usually say I feel sorry for the truck," Buffett sometimes quips. Over the years he's tried various comebacks:[19]

1985: In an article about Berkshire's long-term commitment to the companies it acquires, Buffett noted: "The managers have a corporate commitment and therefore need not worry if my personal participation in Berkshire's affairs ends prematurely (a term I define as any age short of three digits).[20]

1986: "This is the proverbial 'truck' question that I get asked every year. If I get run over by a truck today, Charlie [Munger] would run the business, and no Berkshire stock would need to be sold. Investments would continue."

Also, Buffett surmised that the stock might "move up a quarter or a half point on the day that I go. I'll be disappointed if it goes up a lot."[21]

1991: "Our businesses run as if I'm not there, so the exact location of my body shouldn't matter."[22]

1993: Even the media reminds Buffett of his mortality. A television reporter asked how he'd like to be remembered: "Well, I'd like for the minister to say, 'My God, he was old.'"[23]

1994: "I have publicly announced I plan to run Berkshire until 5 or 10 years after I die. But Berkshire is pretty easy to run."[24]

1995: "I'm thinking of making a purchase of Berkshire," said a member of the audience at the annual meeting, "but

I'm concerned about something happening to you. I cannot afford an event risk."

"Neither can I," Buffett replied.

2000: He wouldn't want to be roadkill, but . . . "Well, just so it's not a GEICO driver."[25]

2006: When Buffett surprised the world with his more than $30 billion charitable giving plan in 2006, shareholders got the message: Buffett acknowledges his mortality, and he's planning ahead. A few years back, Buffett announced that his son Howie would become Berkshire's chairman and that several current managers would take over the operation of the company. It was widely believed that Louis Simpson, who has invested GEICO's insurance float for the last 25 years, would manage much of Berkshire's investments. During his time at GEICO, Simpson outpaced the S&P 500 by almost 7 percent a year, even with some slow years thrown in here and there. The notion that Simpson would take over investments when Buffett could no longer handle them fell by the wayside when, in the 2006 annual report, Buffett wrote that he was accepting resumes from younger candidates for the job. Despite his skills, Simpson is only six years younger than Buffett. Buffett would like to have a succession plan with a longer tail.

## AIM WELL

Invest the same way an expert plays hockey, says Buffett:

> *"Like Wayne Gretzky says, go where the puck is going, not where it is."*[26]

~

> *"To swim a fast 100 meters, it's better to swim with the tide than to work on your stroke."*[27]

## FOCUS ON YOUR GOALS

> *"If we get on the main line, New York to Chicago, we don't get off at Altoona and take side trips."*[28]

~

> *"I've often felt there might be more to be gained by studying business failures than business successes. It's customary in business schools to study business successes. But my partner, Charles Munger, says all he wants to know is where he's going to die—so he won't ever go there."*[29]

## KEEP LIFE IN PERSPECTIVE

Buffett had a notepad on his desk that read:

> *"In the event of nuclear war, disregard this message."*[30]

In 1985, commenting on investments resulting in a 22 percent compounded growth for 20 years:

> *"It has been like overcoming a misspent youth."*[31]

At a cocktail party, a tipsy woman approached Buffett and cooed, "I see money hanging all over you."

Buffett told a reporter:

*"I don't measure my life by the money I've made. Other people might, but I certainly don't."*[32]

~

*"Money, to some extent, sometimes lets you be in more interesting environments. But it can't change how many people love you or how healthy you are."*[33]

~

*"Success is having people love you that you want to have love you."*[34]

~

*"It irritates the hell out of me, but you can't buy love."*[35]

## NICE GUYS FINISH FIRST—SOMETIMES

"We've seen oil magnates, real estate moguls, shippers, and robber barons at the top of the money heap, but Buffett is the first person to get there just by picking stocks," says *Time* reporter John Rothchild.[36] Rothchild failed to mention that Buffett didn't start with inherited money; he made it on his own. Buffett's progression to the top tier of the wealthiest Americans no doubt will become an American legend. Forget Horatio Alger stories. From now on, stories of successful self-made people will be called "Warren Buffett" stories. Step by step, this is how he climbed up the Forbes 400 list of wealthiest Americans, starting in 1943.

1943: Warren tells a pal that he will be a millionaire by age 30 or "I'll Jump off the tallest building in Omaha."[37]

1982: Warren Buffett ranked number 82 with $250 million. Daniel K. Ludwig was first on the list with $2 billion, and Gordon Peter Getty was number 2 with $1.4 billion.

1984: Buffett was number 23 with holdings worth $665 million. First was Getty with $4.1 billion. Second was Sam Walton, worth $2.3 billion.

1985: BUFFETT BECOMES NEBRASKA'S FIRST BILLIONAIRE WITH $1.07 BILLION.[38] He ranked number 12 on the Forbes 400. Walton made the top with $2.8 billion. Ross Perot was number 2 with $1.8 billion.

In 1986, *U.S. News & World Report* published a list of 100 individuals and families who owned the biggest stakes in America's publicly traded companies. Buffett ranked eighth, with the Walton family at the top. Buffett observed: "Did you see how precise they tried to be? The only thing is, they forgot to allow for a couple of burgers that I bought at Bronco's last night."[39]

1988: Buffett's net worth rose to $2.2 billion, but he dropped to ninth place. Walton, with $6.7 billion, and John Kluge, with $3.2 billion, were in the lead.

1989: Buffett sped ahead to number 2 with $4.2 billion. John Kluge was number 1 with $5.2 billion. The leader worldwide was Yoshiaki Tsutsumi, a Japanese developer worth $15 billion.

1991: Lower on the list, but as rich as ever, Buffett took fourth place with $4.2 billion. Kluge again was in first place with $5.9 billion. A newcomer, Bill Gates, took second place with $4.8 billion of net worth.

1993: NUMBER 1 WITH $8.3 BILLION. Bill Gates fell to second-wealthiest American with $6.16 billion.[40]

1994: Back to second place, Buffett's wealth rose to only $9.2 billion. Gates led with $9.35 billion.

On the tug-of-war between Buffett and Gates for first- or second-richest person in the United States, satirist Art Buchwald observed: "Despite being friendly in each other's presence, there must be some tension between the two men. When you're number 1, you're always looking over your shoulder to see who is coming up from behind. On the other hand, when you're number 2, you spend all your time explaining to your family how you failed."[41]

Buffett and Gates took turns being richest man in the world for a few years, then Gates pulled way out in front. In 2006, Gates's net worth was estimated at $50 billion, while Buffett's was only $42 billion. Both men were far ahead of the pack, though. The third-wealthiest person was Carlos Slim Helu of Mexico with $30 million. Alas, in 2007, Slim became number one.

# BE HONEST

Buffett told his son Howard:

> *"It takes 20 years to build a reputation and five minutes to ruin it. If you think about that, you'll do things differently."*[42]

~

> *"Never lie under any circumstances. Don't pay any attention to the lawyers. If you start letting lawyers get into the picture, they'll basically tell you, 'Don't say anything.' You'll never get tangled up if you just basically lay it out as you see it."*

An untruth can be accidental. There *was* the Nicholas Kenner affair. Buffett opened the 1990 annual meeting question-and-answer period by taking an inquiry from the 9-year-old New Yorker who then owned 11 shares of Berkshire. The youngster asked why Berkshire's stock price, at that time trading at about $6,600 per share, was so low. Buffett mentioned the question in his next annual letter to shareholders. Nicholas Kenner appeared at the next annual meeting with an even tougher question. Noting that since the annual report mistakenly said that he was 11, when actually he was 9 years old, Kenner asked, "How do I know the numbers in the back [the financials] are correct?" Buffett promised a written response to the question.[43]

Little white lies are forgiven if they boost the sales of See's Candy, a company owned by Berkhire Hathaway.

*"When business sags, we spread the rumor that our candy acts as an aphrodisiac. Very effective. The rumor, that is; not the candy."*[44]

## TELL THE WHOLE TRUTH, PLEASE

The high standards Buffett holds for journalists go back to his days as a well-organized paperboy. Buffett later became something of an investigative report for a story that won a 1973 Pulitzer prize. It all began in 1969 when Buffett bought the *Sun* newspapers, neighborhood weeklies in Omaha. He had heard rumors that Father Flannigan's Boys Town, at the time a shelter for homeless boys, was amassing large amounts of money from its heart-wrenching pitches and not spending the funds on helping children.

Buffett learned of a new Internal Revenue Service (IRS) regulation requiring charitable foundations to publicly disclose their assets on a Form 990. He talked to the *Sun* staff, who got a copy of the IRS filing that corroborated the rumor. They quietly went to work on the piece, even working from the basement of Buffett's home so that the eight-page story would not leak before it was printed.

Stan Lipsey, publisher of the *Sun* newspapers and later publisher of the *Buffalo News*, explained, "Without Warren there was no story, no Pulitzer. It was his idea; he told us about the Form 990, and then he analyzed the vast Boys Town holdings that totaled $219 million."[45]

Since then Boys Town has regained public trust and has expanded into Girls and Boys Town with facilities in 19 different locations around the country. It remains a leader in the treatment and care of abused, abandoned, and neglected children.

Though he has a lifetime involvement with newspapers, Buffett says dealing with reporters can be risky:

*"The tough part about it is that essentially there is no one, virtually with the exception of an assassin, that can do you as much damage as somebody can in the press, if they do something the wrong way. There may be doctors out there who can do you just as much harm, but in that case, you initiate the transaction."*[46]

One misunderstanding with the media involved the *Lifestyles of the Rich and Famous* television show. Buffett's friends were more than a little surprised when he was featured on Robin Leach's program, since it's not Buffett's habit to parade his wealth.

"I was just as surprised as you were," Buffett reportedly told friends. "I never heard from Robin Leach; we didn't even have a request to appear. Suddenly, we were just on the show."

Leach disputes that version of the story. "Buffett absolutely knew we were doing it. It wasn't a sit-down interview, but he approved. That's why we billboarded the show as an exclusive. It was."

NOTE: Actually Borsheim's jewelry store in Omaha invited *Lifestyles* to film a Patek Phillipe exhibition the Sunday before Berkshire Hathaway's annual meeting. Buffett agreed to talk to Robin Leach in conjunction with the exhibit. A film crew never came to his home, and Buffett was unaware that a show was planned about him.[47]

## LETTER TO THE *WALL STREET JOURNAL*

On August 15, 2003, the *Wall Street Journal* published a front-page story about Buffett and his part in Arnold Schwarzenegger's run for governor of California. (Read more about that on p. 52.) The story implied that Buffett felt California should have higher property taxes, more in line with those in Omaha. In actuality, Buffett was trying to convey the message that property taxes in California were fluky and unfair. The story, with the wrong message, was picked up and repeated around the world. Buffett was not happy about that:

*October 7, 2003*
*Mr. Paul E. Steiger*
*Managing Editor*
*The* Wall Street Journal
*200 Liberty Street*
*New York, New York 10281*

*Dear Mr. Steiger:*

*The* Wall Street Journal's *August 15 article about me, based on an interview that I gave one of your reporters about my association with Arnold Schwarzenegger's campaign, was seriously misleading in a way that caused far-reaching reverberations. For reasons that I will explain, I could not write to you about this matter until now.*

*The article, featured on the* Journal's *front page, carried a headline and opened with paragraphs devoted entirely to California taxes. That's fair enough: Taxes were certainly to be a major issue in the campaign.*

*In talking to your reporter Joe Hallinan, I began by asking him to record the interview. He replied that his taping equipment was not working. Therefore, in verifying with him that what I'm about to recount is correct, you will have to rely on his notes. I do not expect you to find discrepancies, given that he asked me several times to repeat key figures I presented.*

*What I said in respect to property taxes was very specific. I gave him an example of three houses, two in Laguna Beach and one in Omaha. The first Laguna Beach house is a property that I bought in the early 1970s. It has a current market value of about $4 million and, because of the limitations embodied in Proposition 13, carried taxes of only $2,264 in 2003 vs. $2,241 in 2002. The second house, located just in back of the first, is one that I purchased in the mid-'90s. It has a market value of about $2 million and, simply because of its later purchase, carried taxes of $12,002 in 2003 vs. $11,877 in 2002. I pointed out to Joe that these figures mean that the tax rate on the second house—same neighborhood, same owner, same ability to pay—is roughly ten times the rate on the first house.*

*I then referenced my house in Omaha, which I believe to be worth about $500,000 (though it's assessed at about $690,000). Taxes on it were $14,401 in 2003 and $12,481 in 2002.*

*I was satisfied, based on our conversation, that Joe understood the two highly important but uncomplicated points my examples spoke to:*

*1. Residential property taxes in California are wildly capricious, tied as they are to the date of purchase rather than the value of the property or financial circumstances of the owner.*

2. *In the case of properties that a homeowner has held for a long time, residential property tax rates in Omaha are far higher than in California.*

*In the interview, I then said, as the story reported: This property-tax illustration, that tells you, you can draw certain conclusions from that." Give me an F for syntax. Even so, this comment clearly applied to* both *observations regarding property taxes.*

*Yet there was no mention in the story of my second house in Laguna nor* any *mention of the tax inequities within California. Instead, the headline, the body of the story, and quote made it appear as if I was only talking about the differences in taxes between Omaha and California.*

*It's difficult to understand this omission. Imagine that a reporter were to ask a candidate about a fiscal problem and received this reply: "Spending is up 10%, taxes are down 10%—you can draw certain conclusions from that." If the reporter quoted only the tax-change portion on the sentence and followed it with "You can draw certain conclusions from that," readers would be seriously misled.*

*The severe failings in the article were compounded a few days later when the* Journal's *editorial page made the mistake of relying on the accuracy and completeness of the* Journal's *reporting. Though the editorial would have undoubtedly made many of the same points it did had the writer read a complete account of my views, his analysis would have had to be at least somewhat different if he had been aware of both points I made. For example, the statement in the editorial's second paragraph that "no doubt the no-billionaire in Chico will appreciate Mr. Buffett's generosity with their cash flow" would make no sense if the writer had understood I was criticizing the inequities within California. My sympathies are clearly with the "no-billionaire" family purchasing a $300,000 house in Chico today who faces real estate taxes materially higher than those borne by this non-resident billionaire on his $4 million house in Laguna. They, due to Proposition 13, have been selected to subsidize me.*

*The* Journal's *editorial page was not the only medium that drew incorrect and incomplete inferences from the story. The Omaha-Laguna comparison rocketed around the world accompanied by commentary that I was suggesting raising property taxes in California—with no mention at all that I was arguing they needed to be made more equitable. When I subsequently explained to the* Journal's *Kevin Helliker just how misleading the story had been, our office received an e-mail from Joe Hallinan suggesting that I "might be interested in doing another interview with us, expanding on some of his earlier points." It is ironic that the reporter mentioned "expanding" my views when he—or his editor—was the one who had truncated my views in such a misleading and unfair manner. Another interview, of course, would have compounded the problem, since—short of the* Journal *forthrightly acknowledging its original error—it would have appeared that I was scrambling to revise my statement to limit political damage to Arnold. This is the same point, of course, that has deterred me from writing you, or otherwise talking about the tax issues, until we reached a date when my doing so would not influence the election. Because the* Journal's *mischaracterization of my views has achieved such widespread publicity, I am planning to post this letter for an extended period on the Berkshire Hathaway website. In the talks I am periodically asked to give to journalism classes, I will think of this also as a case study of how journalism can go wrong.*

*If the* Journal *has any response to this letter, I will be happy to publish it* in full *on our website and also distribute it to journalism students if I'm using the story as a bad example. If the* Journal *should make any use of this letter, I hope that you, as well, will present it in full, not truncating it in any way.*

*Sincerely,*

*Warren E. Buffett*

# CULTIVATE GOOD CHARACTER

> *"Chains of habit are too light to be felt until they are too heavy to be broken."*[48]

Character can be developed. Imagine, Buffett says, that you are a student and that you may choose one other student in your class and thereafter be entitled to 10 percent of that student's earnings for life. But there's a catch. You also have to choose another student to whom you will pay 10 percent of your earnings for life:

> *"The interesting thing is, when you think about what's going through your mind, you're not thinking about things that are impossible for you to achieve yourself. You're not thinking about who can jump 7 feet, who can throw a football 65 feet, who can recite pi to 300 digits, or whatever it might be. You're thinking about a whole lot of qualities of character. The truth is that every one of those qualities is obtainable. They are largely a matter of habit. My old boss, Ben Graham, when he was 12 years old, wrote down all of the qualities that he admired in other people and all the qualities he found objectionable. And he looked at that list and there wasn't anything about being able to run the 100-yard dash in 9.6 or jumping 7 feet. They were all things that were simply a matter of deciding whether you were going to be that kind of person or not."*[49]

*"Always hang around people better than you and you'll float up a little bit. Hang around with the other kind and you start sliding down the pole."* [50]

## BELIEVE IN YOURSELF

When 20-year-old Buffett went to work at his father's brokerage house in Omaha, a friend asked if the company would be called Buffett & Son. "No," replied Buffett, "Buffett & Father." [51]

In a matter-of-fact way, Buffett says:

*"I've never had any self-doubt. I've never been discouraged."* [52]

~

*"I always knew I was going to be rich. I don't think I ever doubted it for a minute."* [53]

When 26-year-old Warren Buffett created his first partnership in 1956, he told investors:

*"What I'll do is form a partnership where I'll manage the portfolio and have my money in there with you. I'll guarantee you a 5 percent return, and I'll get 20 percent of all profits after that. And I won't tell you what we own because that's distracting. All I want to do is hand in a scorecard when I come off the golf course. I don't want you following me around and watching me shank a three-iron on this hole and leave a putt short on the next one."* [54]

NOTE: Apparently, the preceding is someone's recollection of what Buffett said. Buffett did not guarantee a 5 percent return. The partnership gave the limited partners a preferential return that had to be achieved on a cumulative basis before Buffett earned anything.

> *"I keep an internal scoreboard. If I do something that others don't like but I feel good about, I'm happy. If others praise something I've done, but I'm not satisfied, I feel unhappy."*[55]

When asked how he has the confidence to invest in companies that others shun:

> *"In the end, I always believe my eyes rather than anything else."*[56]

## BUT DON'T GET TOO STUCK ON YOURSELF

Probably the majority of people felt like Buffett did in high school:

> *"I would not have been the most popular guy in the class, but I wouldn't have been the most unpopular either. I was just sort of nothing."*[57]

When Buffett graduated from Columbia, he asked Benjamin Graham for a job (for no salary) at the Graham-Newman Co.:

> *"Ben made his customary calculation of value to price and said no."*[58]

For years, Buffett threw the opening pitch at Omaha Royals games preceding the Berkshire Hathaway annual meetings. Before one game, children asked for his autograph. After his pitch, which was a little weak, Buffett said:

> *"I looked up and saw these same kids erasing my signature."*[59]

Wounded by a journalist who said Buffett wore cheap suits, he explained:

> *"I buy expensive suits. They just look cheap on me."*[60]

NOTE: After years of usually wearing cotton shirts, slacks, and a blazer, Buffett started dressing up. He went to Italian-made Zegna suits, usually off the rack. Zegnas sell for about $2,000.[61]

~

Upon induction to the Omaha Business Hall of Fame, Buffett said he wanted to thank his hair stylist, his wardrobe consultant, and his personal trainer, but:

> *"When they looked at their handiwork, they asked to remain anonymous."*[62]

When the Omaha Press Club unveiled a caricature by artist James Horan, Buffett laughed:

> *"Almost anything beats looking in the mirror."*[63]

Buffett and the governor of Nebraska once performed a skit together, in which the governor announced the winning numbers for a Nebraska state lottery and

Buffett dashed onto stage waving the winning stub. The governor asked Buffett what he would do with the windfall: "I think I'll buy a second suit," the excited Buffett stuttered. He then added, "And if I have enough left over, I'll buy a comb."[64]

Buffett's business partner, Charlie Munger, himself a snappy dresser, says, "Buffett's tailoring has caused a certain amount of amusement in the business world."[65]

When a shareholder asked Buffett if he was aware of how popular he had become, Buffett replied:

*"Maybe I should tell my barber and we should save the clipings."*[66]

When it was suggested to Buffett that, as a folk hero, some people watch his every move:

*"I watch my every move, and I'm not that impressed."*[67]

## CHOOSE YOUR HEROES WELL

"You're lucky in life if you have the right heroes. I advise all of you, to the extent that you can, pick out a few heroes. There's nothing like the right ones," Buffett said.

Among his champions, Buffett lists his father, Howard; Senator Barak Obama; author Phil Fisher; Bill Gates; and his mentor, Ben Graham. Why these people?[68]

# HOWARD HOMAN BUFFETT

"He taught me to do nothing that could [not] be put on the front page of a newspaper. I have never known a better human being than my dad."[69]

Buffett's mother explained the relationship between father and son: "Warren and his father were always the best of friends. His dad was Warren's hero. Howard was a wonderful husband and father. He never found it necessary to punish the children. His method was to use reason and persuasion."[70]

Buffett recalls a hometown baseball game shortly after his father had cast an unpopular House of Representatives vote on a labor measure. When Congressman Buffett was introduced, the crowd booed: "He could take stuff like that very well. He didn't expect the world to change overnight."[71]

Buffett's father was a staunch Republican and a member of the John Birch Society. The senior Buffett had strong and independent views of the role of the United States in the world. In a speech on the House floor, Howard Buffett once said:

> *"Even if it were desirable, America is not strong enough to police the world by military force. If that attempt is made, the blessings of liberty will be replaced by tyranny and coercion at home. Our Christian ideals cannot be exported to other lands by dollars and guns. Persuasion and example are the methods taught by the Carpenter of Nazareth; and if we believe in Christianity, we should try to advance our ideals by his methods."*[72]

Warren eventually abandoned Conservative politics:

*"I became a Democrat basically because I felt the Democrats were closer by a considerable margin to what I felt in the early '60s about civil rights. I don't vote the party line, but I probably vote more for Democrats than Republicans."*[73]

~

*"I'm sort of a Republican on the production side, and I'm sort of a Democrat on the distribution side."*[74]

## SENATOR BARAK OBAMA

*"I've get a conviction about him that I don't get very often. . . . He has as much potential as anyone I've seen to have an important impact over his lifetime on the course that America takes."*[75]

## PHIL FISHER

One of the great original thinkers of modern investment management, Fisher is the author of *Common Stocks and Uncommon Profits* and *Conservative Investors Sleep Well*. Buffett describes his own style as 85 percent Ben Graham and 15 percent Fisher:[76]

*"From him [Fisher] I learned the value of the "scuttlebutt" approach: Go out and talk to competitors, suppliers, customers to find out how an industry or a company really operates."*[77]

NOTE: Fisher's son Kenneth writes a column for *Forbes* magazine.

## BILL GATES

> *"I'm not competent to judge his technical ability, but I regard his business savvy as extraordinary. If Bill had started a hotdog stand, he would have become the hotdog king of the world. He will win in any game. He would be very good at my business, but I wouldn't be at his."*[78]

As for the future of Gates and Microsoft in the shifting sands of computer software, Buffett says:

> *"I'd just bet on him. Nobody has lost money doing that yet."*[79]

NOTE: Buffett did bet on Gates twice and in a big way. First, he invited Gates to serve on Berkshire's board of directors; then, he handed over the bulk of his wealth to the Bill and Melinda Gates Foundation. (For more on that, turn to page 218.)

## BENJAMIN GRAHAM

"Graham was the smartest man I ever knew," Buffett said.[80]

NOTE: Rose Blumkin, founder of the Nebraska Furniture Mart, and all teachers rank high on Buffett's list. More about them later.

## DODGE THE HYPE

*"Maybe grapes from a little eight-acre vineyard in France are really the best in the whole world, but I have always had a suspicion that about 99 percent of it is in the telling and about 1 percent is in the drinking."*[81]

~

In a CNBC interview, Buffett was asked: "You have about $15 billion in cash?" Buffett replied: "Well, I don't have it all on me right now!"[82]

## SHARE YOUR WISDOM

When Bill Gates proposed marriage to Melinda French, he flew his betrothed to Omaha to buy an engagement ring at Borsheim's, a jewelry store owned by Berkshire.

"Not to give you advice or anything," said Buffett, who is known for his unabashed promotion of his own companies, "but when I bought an engagement ring for my wife in 1951, I spent 6 percent of my net worth on it."[83] Though only 37 years old at the time, Gates already was a multibillionaire. Six percent of his net worth would have been around $500 million.

~

Buffett says that he has no political aspirations but that he can help elected officials set better goals. Rather than a balanced budget amendment, he proposes a "3 percent solution":[84]

*"Enact a constitutional amendment stipulating that every sitting representative and senator becomes ineligible for election if in any year of his term our budget deficit runs over 3 percent of the GDP [gross domestic product]. Were this amendment passed, the interests of the nation and the personal interests of our legislators would instantly merge."*

This plan would serve the nation, Buffett says, because:

*"It's not debt per se that overwhelms an individual, corporation, or country. Rather, it is a continuous increase in debt in relation to income that causes trouble."*

Other measures to control the national debt have failed because voters bounce elected officials who actually cut programs or increase taxes:

*"There simply aren't enough saints available to staff a large institution that requires its members to voluntarily act against their own well-being."*

## DISREGARD OLD AGE

*"Retirement plans? About 5 to 10 years after I die."*[85]

Buffett's attitude about his age also applies to those with whom he works:

*"We take as our hero Methuselah."*[86]

Buffett compares the management at Coca-Cola to a winning team:

> *"If you have the 1927 Yankees, all you wish for is their immortality."*[87]

When the now-deceased Rose Blumkin hit 94, Buffett said he was forced to scrap his mandatory retirement-at-100 policy so that Mrs. B could continue to manage the Nebraska Furniture Mart, now owned by Berkshire, from the electric golf cart she steered everywhere.

> *"My god! Good managers are so scarce I can't afford the luxury of letting them go just because they've added a year to their age."*[88]

> *"We find it hard to teach a new dog old tricks. But we haven't had lots of problems with people who hit the ball out of the park year after year. Even though they're rich, they love what they do. And nothing ever happens to our managers. We offer them immortality."*[89]

In recent years Buffett developed a new appreciation for youth. He added both Bill Gates of Microsoft and Susan Decker, chief financial officer of Yahoo!, to the board of directors. Buffett also launched a search for a loyal young genius to help manage Berkshire's investments and possibly become Buffett's successor.

# ROSE BLUMKIN, MATRIARCH OF THE NEBRASKA FURNITURE MART

To Warren Buffett, 4-foot-10-inch, Rose Blumkin was an Omaha landmark. He recommended that visitors drop by and see her when they were in town. Mrs. B, as she was called, founded the massive and modern Nebraska Furniture Mart. Buffett often described her common sense and work ethic when talking to graduate students and others studying business principles. Mrs. B, who never attended a day of school, immigrated from Russia alone at age 23 to join her husband in the United States.

Mrs. B's business motto was "Sell cheap and tell the truth."[90]

"If she ran a popcorn stand, I'd want to be in business with her," Buffett said. He bought the Nebraska Furniture Mart as a 53rd birthday present to himself.[91]

Mrs. B told the story this way: "One day, he [Buffett] walks in and says to me, 'You want to sell me your store?' And I say, 'Yeah.' He says, 'How much do you want?' I say, '$60 million.' He goes to the office and brings back a check. I say, 'You are crazy. Where are your lawyers? Where are your accountants?' He says, 'I trust you more.'"[92]

Later, when an inventory was taken, the store was actually worth $85 million, but Mrs. B did not raise the price.

"I wouldn't go back on my word, but I was surprised. He never thought a minute. But he studies. I bet you he knew."[95]

Buffett had learned of Mrs. B's interest in selling the business and discussed the idea with her son, hoping not to offend Mrs. B when he approached her. The transaction was based on a one-page contract, no audits, and no inventories. The total legal and accounting fees were $1,400. The investment has been hugely successful.[94]

"I would rate him the best," Mrs. B said about Buffett.[95]

Sadly, however, a dispute erupted between Mrs. B and her family. The feud was hot news in Omaha, and the *Omaha World-Herald* reported every lurid detail. "She left the Nebraska Furniture Mart in a major-league snit May 3, 1989, contending that grandsons Ronald and Irvin Blumkin, company executives, were undercutting her authority in the carpet department."[96] The entire family was aghast when Mrs. B called one of her grandsons a "Hitler."

Mrs. B was soon bored sitting at home and, in 1989, opened the six-acre Furniture Warehouse across the street from the Nebraska Furniture Mart. She had no qualms doing this. "Warren Buffett is not my friend. I made him $15 million every year; and when I disagreed with my grandkids, he didn't stand up for me." As for the success of her new business, "I didn't open this store for money. I opened it for revenge."[97]

Mrs. B later made peace with her family and forgave Buffett. She sold her new store and its 11-acre site to the Nebraska Furniture Mart for $4.94 million, putting her back in the fold. As part of the deal, Mrs. B continued to operate her carpet business within the store.

"I expect maybe too much," Mrs. B said of the family fracas. Running the warehouse was a strain, and she sold because her son begged her not to work so hard.

"So I did. Five million dollars. And they paid cash. No credit. I love my kids," she said.

"I'd rather wrestle grizzlies than compete with Mrs. B and her progeny," Buffett said.[98]

Buffett admitted learning an important lesson from the episode. The second time, he asked Mrs. B for a lifetime noncompete clause, remedying a flaw in the Nebraska Furniture Mart purchase agreement of 10 years earlier. "I was young and inexperienced," the 62-year-old Buffett said.[99]

At the Omaha Press Club show in 1987, Buffett sang the following tribute to Rose Blumkin—to the tune of "Battle Hymn of the Republic":

> Oh, we thought we'd make a bundle
> When we purchased ABC.
> But we found it's not so easy
> When your network's number three.
> So now the load at Berkshire
> Must be borne by Mrs. B.
> Her cart is rolling on.

*Chorus:*

Glory, glory, hallelujah

Keep those buyers coming to ya.

If we get rich, it must be through ya,

Her cart is rolling on.

*Verse 2*

Ideas flop and stocks may drop

But never do I pale.

For no matter what my screwups,

It's impossible to fail.

Mrs. B will save me,

She'll just throw another sale.

Her cart is rolling on.

*Verse 3*

*Forbes* may think I'm brilliant

When they make their annual log.

But the secret is I'm not the wheel

But merely just a cog.

Without the kiss of Mrs. B,

I'd always be a frog.

Her cart is roling on.[100]

Rose Blumkin died in 1998 at age 104.

# — About Friends —

## KNOW WHAT FRIENDSHIP IS

*"I have a half dozen close friends. Half male, half female, as it works out. I like them, admire them. There are no shells round them."*[1]

How does Buffett define *friendship*?

*"I remember asking that question of a woman who had survived Auschwitz. She said her test was, 'Would they hide me?'"*[2]

## GO TO BAT FOR YOUR PALS

*"I ate lunch at the Omaha Club—that's the downtown club—and I noticed there weren't any Jews. I was told, 'They have their own club.' Now, there are Jewish families that have been in Omaha a hundred years; they have contributed to the community all the time;*

*they have helped build Omaha as much as anybody; and yet they can't join a club that John Jones, the new middle-rank Union Pacific man, joins as soon as he's transferred here. That is hardly fair. So I joined the Jewish club; it took me four months. They were a little put back and confused, and I had to do some convincing. Then I went back to the Omaha Club and told them that the Jewish club wasn't totally Jewish any more. I got two or three of the Jewish club members to apply to the Omaha Club. Now we've got the thing cracked."*[3]

## GUIDING GOVERNOR SCHWARZENEGGER

Buffett made a political splash in 2003 when he became a volunteer financial adviser to the Republican, former Mr. Universe, kitsch actor Arnold Schwarzenegger in his bid to become governor of California. This was a surprise move for Buffett, who usually votes for Democrats. He did, after all, support Massachusetts senator John Kerry in the 2000 presidential race.

At the time, California had a $38 billion budget deficit and an energy crisis created partly by market manipulation by Enron. Buffett explained:

*"I have known Arnold for years and know he'll be a great governor. It is critical to the rest of the nation that California's economic crisis be solved, and I think Arnold will get that job done."*[4]

Then the playful Buffett kicked in:

> *"Arnold was looking for a double. Maria [Shriver— Schwarzenegger's wife] can't tell us apart."*[5]

"Warren is helping me bring together a world-class team to assist me in addressing the problems and challenges facing businesses, investors, and job creators in California," said Schwarzenegger.[6]

His partnership with his old friend Buffett was hailed as a masterstroke that set him apart from President George W. Bush, who wasn't always popular in California. Yet the alliance soon ran into trouble, such as a misleading story that appeared in the *Wall Street Journal* (see pages 30–35).

Despite glitches, Schwarzenegger got elected and won a second term in 2006. Buffett and his partner, Charlie Munger, supported Schwarzenegger, in part because of his promise to enact Workers' Compensation reform. Workers' Comp abuses had long been the curse of the insurance industry. Between 1997 and 2003, Workers' Comp costs to insurers had more than tripled. Schwarzenegger made Workers' Comp the cornerstone of his first six months in office. Under laws he pushed through, costs to insurers fell by $8.1 billion between 2003 and 2006. Premium rates to businesses dropped by 47 percent.[7]

## BUILD LIFELONG FRIENDSHIPS

In 1968, Buffett and a group of his friends traveled to Coronado, California, where they sought advice on the stock market from their former Columbia professor, Ben Graham. The Buffett Group continues to gather every other year: "They were moderately well-to-do then. They are all rich now. They haven't invented Federal Express or anything like that. They just set one foot in front of the other. Ben put it all down. It's just so simple."[8]

NOTE: Frugal Buffett originally suggested they find a Holiday Inn, but the party stayed at the elegant beachfront Hotel del Coronado.

### CHARLIE MUNGER

Charles T. Munger, 83, is Buffett's combination best friend/business partner. Like Buffett, Munger grew up in Omaha and, as a teenager, worked in Buffett's grandfather Ernest's grocery store.

"The Buffett family store provided a very desirable introduction of business," Munger said. "It required hard, accurate work over long hours, which caused many of the young workers, including me (and later Ernest's grandson Warren), to look for an easier career and to be cheerful upon finding disadvantages therein."[9]

Munger is about seven years older than Buffett, which is one of the reasons the two didn't meet until they were adults. Munger has been called the Buffett doppelgänger, though the description has its limits. Munger was admitted to Harvard Law School even though he didn't have an undergraduate degree; Buffett was rejected when he applied to Harvard Business School. A Republican, Munger gives money liberally to charitable causes, including the British antihunger group, Oxfam. Buffett, a Democrat, has made charitable contributions but hoped to rely on his late wife, Susie, to handle most of that work.

Munger, unlike Buffett, isn't a particular fan of the Benjamin Graham investment philosophy. And yet, says Buffett, "I have been shaped tremendously by Charlie."[10]

Munger explains their synergy: "Everybody engaged in complicated work needs colleagues. Just the discipline of having to put your thoughts in order with somebody else is a very useful thing."[11]

A friend of the partners says that while Buffett is good at saying no, Munger is better. Buffett calls his friend "the abominable no man." To be sure, Munger has mastered short answers. "Charlie is not paid by the word," explains Buffett.[12]

Buffett further claims: "Charlie and I can handle a four-page memo over the phone with three grunts."[13]

Buffett describes his friend as his junior partner in good years and his senior partner in bad years, but that's just talk.[14] "Charlie is rational, very rational. He doesn't have his ego wrapped up in the business the way I do, but he understands it perfectly. Essentially, we have never had an argument, though occasional disagreements."[15]

Furthermore: "Charlie has the best 30-second mind in the world. He goes from A to Z in one move. He sees the essence of everything before you even finish the sentence."[16]

Buffett says it isn't necessary to be a rocket scientist to be a successful investor, though in Munger's estimation, Warren is plenty smart: "His brain is a superbly rational mechanism. And since he's articulate, you can see the damn brain working."[17]

Munger says Buffett is the same person in private that he is in public: "One of the reasons Warren is so cheerful is that he doesn't have to remember his lines."[18]

Munger says he can't recall Buffett ever getting angry: "Even when I took him fishing in Minnesota and upset the boat and we had to swim to shore, he didn't scream at me."[19]

When he gets around to talking, Munger has good advice for investors: "There are huge advantages for an individual to get into a position where you make a few great investments and just sit back. You're paying less to brokers. You're listening to less nonsense."[20]

～

Munger wants more than rosy promises before Berkshire Hathaway invests in a company. Projections won't do:

"They are put together by people who have an interest in a particular outcome, have a subconscious bias, and [their] apparent precision makes them fallacious. They remind me of Mark Twain's saying, 'A mine is a hole in the ground owned by a liar.' Projections in America are often lies, although not intentional ones, but the worst kind because the forecaster often believes them himself." [21]

Bull markets, Munger says, go to investor's heads: "If you're a duck on a pond, and it's rising due to a downpour, you start going up in the world. But you think it's you, not the pond." [22]

Munger isn't above a bit of silliness. When asked if he could play the piano: "I don't know. I've never tried." [23]

Munger say he and Buffett think so much alike that it's spooky. [24] Some of the differences between them, however, are striking: "In my whole life, nobody has ever accused me of being humble. Although humility is a trait I much admire, I don't think I quite got my full share." [25]

# — About Family —

## DON'T SPOIL YOUR KIDS

First of all a clarification—Warren Buffett and musician Jimmy Buffett of "Margaritaville" fame probably are not related. If there is a kinship, it's buried so deep in the bloodline that nobody can find it. But there is one connection—Jimmy is a Berkshire investor.

~

One of the great transformations in Buffett's life over the past decade has occurred within his family. His wife, Susie, was battling mouth cancer when she suddenly died of a stroke. Two years later, Warren and his companion, Astrid Menks, were married. And in a seemingly natural way, each of his children has progressively defined and strengthened her or his own role in the world. There now is a clearer picture of how the Buffett offspring conduct themselves, considering that they are surely among the most privileged people on earth.

While the younger Buffetts cannot be accurately described in simple terms, I will try. Suzie tends to keep the Nebraska home fires burning; Howard is the fiscally conservative international environmentalist and Berkshire heir apparent; and Peter is the musical, creative dreamer.

～

Munger explains Buffett's attitude regarding family: "Warren is just as tough on his children as he is on his employees. He doesn't believe that if you love somebody the way to do him good is to give him something he's not entitled to. And that's part of the Buffett personality."[1]

*"Our kids are great. But I would argue that when your kids have all the advantages anyway, in terms of how they grow up and the opportunities they have for education, including what they learn at home—I would say it's neither right nor rational to be flooding them with money. Dynastic megawealth would further tilt the playing field that we ought to be trying instead to level."*[2]

Buffett calls inherited wealth "food stamps for the rich."

*"All these people who think that food stamps are debilitating and lead to a cycle of poverty, they're the same ones who go out and want to leave a ton of money to their kids."*[3]

Eldest son Howard explained: "Listen, anybody who doesn't think my Dad is smart—as soon as he started giving us allowance, he put a slot machine up in the attic; and we'd go up there, and he'd win every penny back of the allowance. In 10 years, I couldn't get three of those melons to line up."[4]

Rumors that Buffett cut his children out of his will are incorrect:

> *"They've gotten gifts right along, but they're not going to live the life of the superrich. I think they probably feel pretty good about how they've been brought up. They all function well, and they are all independent, in that they don't feel obliged to kowtow to me in any way."*[5]

In her book *Buffettology* (Scribner, 1997), Mary Buffett described Christmas mornings when Warren stuffed stockings with $10,000 worth of stock in companies he found promising. Father Buffett urged the family to use the shares wisely to build their own investment portfolios.

After explaining his family philosophy to a group of college students, Buffett conceded:

> *"My kids will be glad to come and rebut this next week."*[6]

Suzie Buffett had a response: "The truth is, it would be insane to leave us that much money. It just would be."[7]

Buffett believes his child-rearing practices brought good results:

> *"They've all gone their own ways to accomplish a lot. They're productive, and they don't expect to just be some rich guy's kid."*[8]

When Buffett's son Howard ran for county commissioner in Omaha, voters falsely assumed that with his surname, his campaign would be well financed. On the contrary, Buffett said:

*"I asked him to spell his name in lowercase letters so that everyone would realize that he was the Buffett without the capital."*[9]

NOTE: Howard was elected and served as Douglas County Commissioner from 1989 to 1992.

Buffett gave Howard a break when, after he dropped out of the University of California-Irvine, Warren got him a job at See's Candy. There, Howie met his future wife, Devon.

~

This little item was found in an *Outstanding Investor Digest* interview with Buffett's friend, superinvestor Walter Schloss:

"We understand that Peter Kiewit . . . had a father who felt the same way as Buffett does about the evils of inherited wealth," said the interviewer.

"As we recall, much to Peter Kiewit Jr.'s surprise some years after his father's death, he received a delayed, out-of-the-blue inheritance of a few million dollars. While it was peanuts compared to the estate his father had built and relative to the success he himself achieved, he said it made him feel like his father was extending his approval from the grave."[10]

NOTE: Until Peter Kiewit's death, he was Omaha's wealthiest and most prominent citizen. Buffett's offices are in Kiewit Plaza.

It is highly likely that the Buffett children someday will also inherit from their father, since his personal investments, those held outside Berkshire Hathaway, have also compounded, although Buffett's true net worth is not publicly known.

*"[W]ay back when I was buying Berkshire, I had less than $1 million in outside cash. Well, I've made a few decent investments with that money in the years since— taking positions that were two small for Berkshire, doing some fixed-income arbitrage, and selling my interest in a bank that was split off from Berkshire."*[11]

# THE BUFFETT CHILDREN

## Susan A. Buffett (Little Suzie)

Suzie Junior was a typical child in many ways: "When I was little, every night my Dad rocked me to sleep and sang 'Somewhere over the Rainbow.'"[12] Little did she suspect that there would be a real pot of gold at the end of the rainbow.

Certainly she did not realize she had an unusual father: "For years I didn't even know what he did. They asked me at school what he did, and I said he was a security analyst; and they thought he checked alarm systems."[13]

Even after Buffett became famous, Suzie said he remained an everyday guy. "What makes my Dad happy is hanging around the house, reading, playing bridge, and talking with us. He's about as normal as you can get."[14]

As for his attitude about investing, "The whole thing is a big game to him. Dollars are the mark of the winner. He doesn't spend anything. He'll drive his car and wear his clothes until they fall apart."[15]

Suzie, 54 years old and the divorced mother of two grown children, lives in Omaha only blocks from her father. Although she usually is described as a homemaker, Suzie has been involved with various small businesses, including a knitting shop and an organization that provides Berkshire logo wear. She loves to sew, quilt, and knit. She often helps her father with corporate entertainment and accompanies him on his travels. Nevertheless, when Suzie goes to Borsheim's jewelry store to make an exchange, she stands in line at the service desk like all the other customers. That's the way it is in the Buffett household.

For years, Suzie was frustrated by the mistaken impression people had of her personal wealth, especially when she was asked to contribute to charitable causes. "They don't understand that when I write my Dad a check for $20, he cashes it. If I had $2,000 now, I'd pay off my credit card bill."[16]

That situation gradually changed, first when Buffett established the Sherwood Trust (named after Robin Hood's forest) and deposited $500,000 per year to it so that his children and his companion, Astrid Menks, could make their own contributions without checking in with him. Finally, Warren and his late wife established charitable trusts for each of their children. In 2006, Buffett made the children's foundations even larger.

Her father wrote to Suzie when he enlarged the trust:

*"I am enormously proud of the way in which you have managed the resources of the foundation that Mom and I established for you. Your thinking has been good, and your actions have been effective in helping those less fortunate than our family have been."*[17]

Suzie's foundation is modest in comparison to the Gates Foundation. The Susan A. Buffett Foundation had assets of $118 million in 2006. The trust eventually will get another $50 billion from Susie Sr.'s estate. Warren then gifted each of his children's trusts with 350,000 Berkshire Hathaway B shares. Based on the June 2006 share price of $3,047, that means Suzie eventually will have more than $1.5 billion to give away.

When making the donations to his children, Buffett recalled the story of how Ted Turner trembled when he gave a large portion of his net worth to the United Nations. Buffett said he had no such trouble when putting money in his children's foundations.

*"It's easy to sign. I just signed 'Dad.'"*

Buffett was glad to let his children make their own decisions about the money:

*"I think their judgment above the ground is going to be a lot better than mine six feet below the ground."*[18]

How will Suzie use the gift? She most likely will continue with the type of volunteer work she's always done. Suzie led the effort to create the Rose Blumkin Theater in downtown Omaha. Like her parents, she supports reproductive rights and family planning organizations, such as Planned Parenthood of Nebraska-Council Bluffs. She serves on the board of Girls Inc. Focusing her attention mainly on Nebraska, Suzie has funded ceiling repairs at St. Cecilia's elementary school, Christian Urban Education, Countryside Community Church, the Special Olympics, and foster-care grants.

## Howard Graham Buffett

Buffett's first son is named for two important role models in Warren's life: his father, Howard, and his teacher and mentor, Benjamin Graham. Not only does Howard's name signify the affection and the respect Warren had for two remarkable men, but it also implies high expectations.

A college dropout like his brother and sister, Howard nonetheless is the nearest thing to a successor that Warren has. He is the man that shareholders watch. Howard is the only one of the Buffett children to serve on the Berkshire board of directors; and, more important, he has been tagged to become chairman of Berkshire when Warren can no longer serve.

Clearly, Howard has been prepping for the day when he carries his father's flag. He worked at ConAgra Foods as vice president and assistant to the chairman and now sits on the ConAgra board of directors. He formerly served on the board of Archer Daniels Midland (ADM), leaving after a price-fixing scandal that did not involve him. Currently, he is chairman of Lindsay Manufacturing Co., an Omaha-based corporation that makes agricultural irrigation systems, controls, and similar equipment. For a while he replaced his father on the board of Coca-Cola Enterprises Inc., a company in which Berkshire has large and neigh onto permanent holdings. Howard since has resigned from the Coca-Cola board.

A true midwesterner, Howard and his wife, Devon, and their five children live on their 850-acre corn and soy bean farm near Decatur, Illinois.

Howie Buffett's claim that he is a Republican causes some conservatives to choke on pretzels. "Even though Howard Buffet is supposed to be a Republican, it does not appear that his own Howard G. Buffett Foundation funds any Republican or conservative causes."[19]

Most of Howard's charitable giving goes to the environment. Howard comes alive when he talks about conservation and wildlife. His nature photographs have appeared in *National Geographic*, and he has published half a dozen photography books. He helped establish the South Africa–based Nature Conservation Trust and is on the board of the Cougar Fund, which protects mountain lions in the United States. Mostly, however, Howard focuses on international rather than domestic causes. Each year, for example, the $25,000 *National Geographic*/Buffett award is presented to someone who has advanced the understanding and practice of conservation in southern Africa and East Africa.

The Howard Buffett Foundation was established in 1999 and had $130 million in assets at the time of his father's pledge of more than $1 billion in 2006. The settlement of his mother's estate will boost the foundation even more. In 2005, Howard distributed $6 million to charitable organizations, an amount that could explode to annual contributions of more than $55 million.

While in the past his passion has been saving wild creatures such as cheetahs, bald eagles, African gorillas, and pandas in China, this is shifting. His attention has moved to human trafficking and to the people in areas where plants, animals, and the environment are under stress, including the U.S./Mexico border and the African nation of Darfur: "I ended up seeing that you can't do anything in conservation work unless you take care of human issues first," Howard explained. "A friend of mine once said, 'You're not going to get someone to starve to save a tree.'"[20]

## Peter Buffett

The youngest and hippest of the Buffett children, Peter, 49, took his mother's musical talent and revved it up. He's a keyboardist and composer of New Age music, most notably film scores and commercials. Under contracts to Narada, Epic, and Hollywood Records, he has produced music that best can be explained as energetic, fluid, and forward moving. It has been described as having catlike qualities, and Peter admits to composing music with a cat wandering around his studio. He created the fire song for *Dances with Wolves* and songs for *The Scarlet Letter.* His production *Spirit,* inspired by Native American music and dancing and performed along with native talent, aired as a public television fundraiser and was heard at the opening of the Smithsonian's Native American Museum in Washington, D.C.

He and his second wife, Jennifer, lived in Milwaukee until 2005, when they moved to New York. Peter's first wife, Mary, coauthored (with David Clark) the books *Buffettology* (Scribner, 1997) and *The Tao of Warren Buffett* (Scribner, 2006), based on investing tips she picked up as a member of the Buffett family.

Peter started his charitable work with his Spirit Foundation but later renamed it NoVo, for the Latin word meaning "to change, alter, invent."

Like the other Buffett foundations, Peter's NoVo is getting $50 million from his mother's estate. With his father's 2006 $1 million pledge, Peter's grants could nearly double, although it will be 20 years before the foundation receives all the money it has coming.

While Warren's donations are designated for charitable causes, both Peter and Jennifer work 30 hours each week for NoVo, for which they receive annual incomes of $40,000. Despite their salaries, administrative expenses for NoVo in 2005 were only $308,498, relatively small for a foundation of its size.

In 2006, Peter and Jennifer contributed $10.7 million in grants to 88 different charities, with an emphasis on Native American causes. One small grant helped a Canadian Indian tribe get back a totem pole that had made its way to Sweden. Each year, Peter's and Howard's foundations join forces to present a deserving Native American with the $25,000 Buffett Award for Indigenous Leadership. In the Milwaukee area, where Jennifer (Heils) comes from an old-line industrial family, the couple has focused on child care centers, early childhood education, and access to family planning for those with low incomes. Like other Buffett family trusts, NoVo's work doesn't please everyone. NoVo took a lot of flak from conservatives for helping fund the Rainforest Action Network, an organization that, among other things, put pressure on Home Depot to stop selling wood products from endangered forests.

## WHAT OTHERS SAY ABOUT WARREN BUFFETT

### Governor Arnold Schwarzenegger

"Warren has a common sense approach to business issues and an integrity that is unmatched. That's the same way I want to approach governing. Warren always tells it the way it is."[21]

### "Doc" William Angle

Doc Angle was one of Omaha's "Buffett millionaires." An early investor, he placed just over $10,000 with Buffett in the 1950s. By the early 1990s, that investment had grown to more than $100 million. Angle died several years ago, but his family still owns shares.

"Warren may seem easygoing, but nothing upsets him like losing money—he loves winning. He loves the game. The end is always the money—not to spend it, of course, but to accumulate it."[22]

## WALTER SCHLOSS

Buffett met Walter Schloss when they both were students at Columbia University. Later, the two worked together at Graham-Newman Co. Schloss then left to open his own investment firm. Buffett has called him a "superinvestor of Graham & Doddsville." Schloss recalled the young Buffett:

"One of the reasons why Warren is such an attractive personality is that he has such a great sense of humor and all those terrific stories. But apparently he was shy when he was young and decided that he wanted to overcome it. So he went to the Dale Carnegie course. . . .

"I saw him in Omaha back in 1961 or 1962 when he got up before a Rotary Club and gave a brilliant speech culminating in asking for money. He was the youngest person there, and it was very, very funny. I wish I had a tape recorder. It was great."[23]

~

As to the high share price of Berkshire Hathaway stock, Schloss says it's far smarter to multiply the number of Berkshire shares outstanding by the share price, then compare that to other companies of similar size in terms of revenues and assets.

"People do not take into consideration the market value of a company they're buying. They just look at the price per share rather than the value of the company."[24]

## PHIL CARRET

Carret was one of the successful long-term investors described by John Train in *The New Money Masters*. Right up to his death, Carret seldom missed Berkshire's annual meeting. Of Buffett, he said:

"He's a friend of mine. He's smarter than I am. He proved that in General Foods. It was a stodgy company, mostly coffee. When Berkshire Hathaway bought the stock, I said to myself, 'Well, Warren's made a mistake this time; it was about $60 when I noticed the transaction. In a matter of months, it went to $120 . . . ha, ha!' (Carret had a deep, throaty chuckle when he told stories of this sort. He particularly enjoyed tales describing common opinions that are completely mistaken.)"[25] Carret's book *The Art of Speculation* (Barron's, 1927), is considered a classic.

## BILL GATES, WORLD'S GREATEST ENTREPRENEUR

Gates's mother invited him to a day-long picnic at which she planned to introduce her son to Buffett, his rival as the wealthiest person in the United States. Gates balked, thinking he had little to say to a man who did nothing but invest all day long. He decided to go when he heard that Katharine Graham, former publisher of the *Washington Post*, also would attend.

When Gates and Buffett met, they fell into conversation and soon became buddies. Buffett attended Gates's wedding in Hawaii; later, Warren and Susan Buffett joined

Gates on a tour of China. Though Gates describes their talks as "candid and not at all adversarial," they do "joust now and then" over mathematics.

Gates says Buffett once challenged him to a game of dice, using a set of four unusual dice with a combination of numbers from 0 to 12 on the sides. Buffett suggested that each of them choose one of the dice, then discard the other two. They would bet on who would roll the highest number most often. Buffett said Gates could pick his die first. This suggestion instantly roused Gates's curiosity. He asked to examine the dice, after which he demanded that Buffett choose first.

"It wasn't immediately evident that because of the clever selection of numbers for the dice, they were non-transitive," Gates said. "The mathematical principle of transivity—that if A beats B and B beats C, then A beats C—did not apply. Assuming dies were rerolled, each of the four dice could be beaten by one of the others: Die A would beat B an average of 11 out of every 17 rolls—almost two-thirds of the time. Die B would beat C with the same frequency. Likewise, C would beat D 11/17 of the time, too. And improbable as it sounds, die D would beat A just as often."[26]

## JOHN TRAIN, AUTHOR OF *THE NEW MONEY MASTERS*

Said Train of Buffett, "Professionally, he is in the vulture business, but he is a cheerful sort of vulture."[27]

## Jack Byrne, Former Chairman of GEICO

Byrne and a group of golfing buddies were on an outing at Pebble Beach, California, when the group playfully offered Buffett a bet: his $10 against their $20,000 that he couldn't score a hole in one over the next three days. Everyone but Buffett agreed to the wager.

"Well, we heaped abuse on him and tried to cajole him—after all it was only $10," Byrne said. "But he said he thought it over and decided it wasn't a good bet for him. He said if you let yourself be undisciplined on the small things, you'd probably be undisciplined on the large things, too."[28]

## Lally Weymouth, Writer (and Daughter of Katherine Graham)

"I think the secret of his success is his undiminished curiosity."[29]

## Chuck Huggins, Head of See's Candy

"When I talk to him, he's always up, always positive."[30]

## Dennis Eckart, Ohio Congressman

At a 1991 Congressional hearing on the Salomon government securities trading incident, Eckhart applauded Buffett for taking responsibility: "Gordon Gekko and Sherman McCoy are alive and well on Wall Street. Mr. Buffett, get in there and kick some butt."[31]

## Irving Kahn, New York Investment Manager

Kahn served for many years as Ben Graham's classroom assistant at Columbia University. He first met Buffett there. "He was much the same as he is now, but he was a brash, cocky young guy—he was always busy on his own. He has tremendous energy. He could wear you out talking to you. He was very ambitious about making money."[32]

### SWOOZIE KURTZ, ACTRESS (AND DISTANT RELATIVE AND FRIEND)

"People still think Warren is this bumpkin from Omaha. And he'd just as soon let them think that. But nothing could be further from the truth. He's an enormously sophisticated man."[33]

### ANTHONY ABBOTT, OWNER OF THE FRENCH CAFE, OMAHA

Maybe, Abbott suggests, we get the Warren Buffett we demand: "Warren is a hero, and people like their myths neat and uncomplicated. Of course, none of this is uncomplicated."[34]

## WORK THINGS OUT WITH YOUR WIFE

Buffett, who speaks tenderly of his late wife, once described Susan T. Buffett this way: "She sort of roams. She's a free spirit."[35]

Even though Warren and Susie had lived apart since 1977 when she moved to San Francisco, they never divorced and often traveled and attended family events together. Susie served on the board of Berkshire Hathaway and held 2.2 percent of the company, or $3 billion worth of shares, in her own name.

In 2003, Susie was diagnosed with mouth cancer and had been treated by surgery and radiation. On July 29, 2004, while she and Warren were visiting friends in Cody, Wyoming, Susie suffered a stroke. Warren was with her in the hospital when she died.

Susie's death changed everything for Buffett. He seemed to realize that all things are fleeting, even himself. He then began a process of change that altered his daily life, his work life, and his afterlife.

~

Around the time her youngest child was graduating from high school, Susie Buffett launched a nightclub singing career. She told a reporter: "I'm really proud of myself. Because there's nothing I would be more vulnerable about trying than singing. Nothing. I'm so proud that I did it. I can't believe I did."[36]

Her husband, Susie said, encouraged her: "It was Warren. He's the one. He knew. He said to me, 'Susie, you're like somebody who has lost his job after 23 years. Now what are you going to do?' He knew I wanted to sing. But I was scared to death."[37]

And what was Buffett's motive? "Warren understands me. And he wants me to stay alive. If you love someone, you do."[38]

Family friend Eunice Denenberg saw Susie Buffett this way: "Susie is one of those old-fashioned *good* people that lots of folks today don't think exist. So they attribute some of their own baser behavior to her because it bothers them."[39]

The story goes that Warren was so sad after Susie left Omaha that she contacted her friend Astrid Menks and asked her to go cook him some soup or something and cheer him up. Astrid, an attractive blonde, soon became Warren's companion and housekeeper. They lived together for 25 years and were married two and a half years after Susie died.

Buffett had always said that on his passing, his fortune would go to the Buffett Foundation, which he expected Susie to direct. After her death, he came up with a better idea, which took the world completely by surprise. In her honor, he renamed the foundation as the Susan T. Buffett Foundation and contributed about $3 billion in the form of Berkshire Hathaway B shares to it. The foundation will receive 5 percent of the shares until they are gone. He also gave some money to his children's foundations, but he turned the largest portion over to the Bill and Melinda Gates Foundation, making it by far the world's largest and most influential charitable organization. (You can read more about his gifts in the pages ahead.)

In the meantime, the world joined Warren in mourning the loss of his wife, whom many felt they knew following a Charlie Rose Public Television interview. On that show, Susie expressed a simple life philosophy:

"Show up, listen hard, don't lie, do your best, and don't be attached to the results."

Susan Buffett was 72 when she died and was the seventeenth-richest woman in the world.[40] She left an estate valued at $2.6 billion. The rock singer Bono performed at her funeral, singing "Forever Young" and "All I Want Is You." Bono had gotten to know Susie through her charitable work. He thanked her for her contributions in the liner notes of his 2004 CD, *How to Dismantle an Atomic Bomb*.

## ASTRID MENKS, BUFFETT'S SECOND WIFE

Neither Astrid Menks nor Buffett discussed their relationship much, though Buffett admits the triangular arrangement with his wife Susan was unusual.

"If you knew everybody well, you'd understand it quite well,"[41] Buffett said.

Back when she was still Buffett's housekeeper, Menks said: "I have the best of all worlds, and I wouldn't change anything."

As to a reporter who attempted to demean her by referring to her as a "former waitress" or "supper club hostess," she is reported to have replied: "Look, I don't want to be lumped in with those kinds of women. I've been with Warren for 13 years [since 1978]. I'm no bimbo, and I'm no airhead."[42]

NOTE: There is some question about the accuracy of this quote. Menks apparently was baited into a response by a reporter, and the story that followed did not reflect her feelings. She says that, in fact, she respects waitresses, just as she would any other woman working for a living.

~

The afternoon of August 30, 2006, Warren's seventy-sixth birthday, some of Buffett's colleagues were surprised to get an e-mail from him. It informed them that he would be in the office until midafternoon. At 6 P.M., he would wed Astrid Menks, but he would be back at work the usual time the next day.

The 15-minute wedding was unpretentious. It was held at the home of Warren's daughter and performed by a local judge. Mostly likely the ring was not unpretentious. With the help of his daughter Suzie, Warren selected it at Borsheim's Fine Jewelry (owned by Berkshire). This is the same establishment where Bill Gates purchased Melinda's ring.

After formalizing Warren and Astrid's 20-year relationship, the wedding party celebrated with dinner at Bonefish Grill in Omaha.

## THE CONTROVERSIAL SUSAN T. BUFFETT FOUNDATION

Each year at the Berkshire Hathaway annual meeting, picketers pace in front of the meeting hall and again at Gorat's

Steak House, carrying placards showing aborted fetuses and decrying the Buffetts as murderers for their passionate support of reproductive rights and population issues.

The Susan T. Buffett (STB) Foundation reportedly helped the Center for Reproductive Rights pay for the battle to reverse Nebraska's ban on the so-called "partial birth" abortion. The campaign succeeded in 2001. The foundation also helped fund the RU-468 "day-after abortion pill" and supplied funds to Planned Parenthood Federation of America, the Population Council, Catholics for a Free Choice, and the National Campaign to Prevent Teen Pregnancy.

The Susan T. Buffett Foundation has also given money to hospitals, universities, teachers, and student scholarships. This includes $10 million each to Save the Children and to Bono's charity for Africa relief, DATA. Susie donated $5 million to her old school, Omaha Central High School, for a new stadium and another $6 million to five California doctors for the study of mouth cancer.

STB in 2006 had more than $318 million in assets. The foundation will receive $2.5 billion in Berkshire shares from Susie's estate and will eventually get $3 billion from Warren. It is the foundation's intention to make grants of around $150 million each year. It is estimated that STB will reach $5 billion, putting it among the top 20 U.S. foundations.[43]

STB is run by Allen Greenberg, former husband of Buffett's daughter Suzie. In a letter to the board of directors after his first wife's death, Buffett reconfirmed his support of the STB Foundation. "Under Allen's leadership, the foundation has succeeded beyond our high expectations— delivering enormous results per dollar spent."[44]

## BE KIND TO YOUR MOTHER

Some authors have described Buffett's mother, Leila, as moody and difficult to grow up with. Buffett speaks affectionately of her. He was generous with the 92-year-old widow and sometimes introduced her at annual meetings. He once bought himself an exercise bike and bought another one (along with a new car) for his mom:

> "Between the two of us, we put 25,000 miles on those machines. But all the mileage was on hers . . . I should have bought her a bicycle, instead of a Cadillac."[45]

Buffett's mother shed more light on the situation: "Warren gave me a Cadillac for my 80th birthday. I've got only 8,000 miles on it. But I've put 19,190 miles on my Exercycle."[46]

~

Likewise, Buffett appreciates the gifts his mother gave to him:

> "My health is terrific. I just went for the first time in six or seven years for a general checkup. The doctor asked me about my diet and said, 'You're counting rather heavily on your genes, aren't you?'"[47]

# WHAT LEILA BUFFETT HAD TO SAY ABOUT HER SON

In junior high school Buffett wasn't a top scholar, though his mother said his poor grades were only temporary: "I think Warren was just going through a phase at the time. He always got very good grades before and after that. He was a good boy. Easy to raise. He never gave us any trouble at all. He never smoked or drank."[48]

When asked if she knew her son would someday accumulate so much wealth: "Oh my, no; I never dreamed that would happen. But Warren always had a fascination for numbers in connection with earning money."[49]

His mother valued Buffett for himself rather than his wealth: "I'm more proud of him for the kind of human being he has become. He's wonderful person."[50]

NOTE: Leila Buffett passed away on Warren's birthday, August 30, 1996. She was 92.

# WHAT THE CRITICS SAY

Despite his reputation as a straight shooter, Buffett has critics. The *Wall Street Journal*[51] accused him of taking advantage of his reputation and wealth to secure deals that other investors cannot get: "By offering help against takeover attacks to USAir, Gillette, and Salomon, he has managed to extract exclusive and highly favorable investment deals for his Berkshire Hathaway investment company that weren't available to other shareholders; these three deals alone total $1.7 billion."

And later in the same story: "Mr. Bufett has 'done a brilliant job of convincing people' that his white squire investments are good for America, says a well-known raider. But the jury is still out on whether the companies are being smart in forging protection arrangements with Mr. Buffett."

NOTE: Buffett later was forced to take a management role at Salomon to help the company recover from an episode of illegal government bond trading; he also had to take a write-down of $268.5 million on the USAirways investment. Buffett began pulling out of those two companies when the opportunity arose. Ultimately, Berkshire Hathaway did not actually experience a loss on USAirways. Not only did the securities return to the price Buffett paid for them, but USAirways, declared a substantial dividend. Buffett no longer holds investments in USAirways. Gillette was acquired by Procter & Gamble in 2005.

## SIR JAMES GOLDSMITH, BRITISH INDUSTRIALIST

"I don't understand people like Warren Buffett who pride themselves on living in their first house and driving a used Chevy to work, despite being billionaires."

After that quote ran in *Time* magazine, Goldsmith called Buffett and apologized, implying that he was misquoted.[52]

## ALLEN GREENE, COPY EDITOR AND LATER UNION PRESIDENT, THE *BUFFALO NEWS*

When asked in 1982 if the *Buffalo News* could initiate a profit-sharing plan, considering its high profitability, Buffett is said to have replied: "There's nothing you people on the third floor [the newsroom] do that has any effect on my profits, so I don't feel any desire to share them with you."

Greene said of the *Buffalo News* staff, "We were stunned. We thought he was such a nice guy." [53]

NOTE: Stan Lipsey, publisher of the *Buffalo News,* says he was present at all meetings Buffett had with union members, and he does not remember Buffett making this comment. Buffett may have made a general statement about the economics of newspapers that dominate a market, which may have been interpreted this way by Greene, Lipsey says. Greene stands behind his statement.

## MICHAEL LEWIS, AUTHOR

Not everyone thinks Buffett is a genius; and former Salomon trader and author of *Liar's Poker* (Norton, 1989), Michael Lewis, seem to be one of them. "He regularly ridicules skeptical professors with a vaguely thuggish if-you're-so-smart-why-am-I-rich routine. (The reason he is rich is simply that random games produce big winners, but pity the business school professor on $50 grand a year who tries to argue with a billionaire.)" [54]

# About Work

Philosophers tell us to do what we love and success will follow. Buffett is living proof that it works.

## WORK FOR THE FUN OF IT

Warren Buffett noted that when he graduated from Columbia University:

> *"Wall Street [in 1951] wasn't a hot place to work at all. The Dow was 200, and the market from 1945 to 1949 had gone sort of sideways. The high was about 190, and the low was about 160. Then it started moving up; 1950 was the first year the Dow never sold below 200. In 1929, it sold at 381; but during the year, it was below 200. So people were very suspicious about the postwar [era] and thought we were going into a depression. [Wall Street] was not a big money place to work . . . it was quite a different world."[1]*

Buffett says working with people you don't like is like "marrying for money":

*"I think that's kind of a crazy way to live. It's probably a bad idea under any circumstances, but absolutely nuts if you're already rich."*[2]

~

*"What I am is a realist. I always knew I'd like what I'm doing. Oh, perhaps it would have been nice to be a major league baseball player, but that's where the realism comes in."*[3]

~

*"It's not that I want money. It's the fun of making money and watching it grow."*[4]

~

*"I'm the luckiest guy in the world in terms of what I do for a living. No one can tell me to do things I don't believe in or things I think are stupid."*[5]

Buffett is often encouraged to run for political office:

*"I wouldn't trade my job for any job, and that includes political life."*[6]

Buffett describes Berkshire Hathaway as "my canvas."[7]

*"I have a blank canvas and a lot of paint, and I get to do what I want. Now there is more money and things*

*are on a bigger scale, but I had just as much fun 10 or 20 years ago when it was on a smaller scale."*[8]

~

*"When I go to my office every morning, I feel like I'm going to the Sistine Chapel to paint."*[9]

~

*"[I] enjoy the process far more than the proceeds, though [I] have learned to live with those also."*[10]

Buffett's maternal grandfather owned a newspaper, and Warren earned much of his early income as a carrier for the *Washington Post* and as circulation manager for the *Lincoln Journal*. Newspapers are in his blood:

*"Let's face it, newspapers are a hell of a lot more interesting business than, say, making couplers for rail cars. While I don't get involved in the editorial operations of the papers I own, I really enjoy being part of the institutions that help shape society."*[11]

~

*"My guess is that if Ted Williams was getting the highest salary in baseball and he was hitting .220, he would be unhappy. And if he was getting the lowest salary in baseball and batting .400, he'd be very happy. That's the way I feel about doing this job. Money is a*

*by-product of doing something I like doing extremely well."* [12]

~

*"I feel like tap dancing all the time."* [13]

## START EARLY

Buffett bought his first stock at age 11 when he and his sister Doris bought three shares of Cities Service preferred stock for $38 per share. He also learned a lesson about patience. When the stock fell to $27, they became a little concerned. After Cities Service rallied to $40, they sold the shares but the stock price kept going— eventually climbing to $200 per share.

> *"I'd been interested in the stock market from the time I was 11, when I spent some time watching the market and marking the board at Harris Upham, a New York Stock Exchange firm that was in the same building as my dad's firm, Buffett-Falk & Co."* [14]

Throughout his childhood, Buffett got involved in many businesses. He sold Cokes at a markup to his friends, published a race track tip sheet, carried newspapers, and recycled golf balls. While at Woodrow Wilson High School in Washington, he and a friend bought a reconditioned pinball machine for $25. Operating as the Wilson Coin Operated Machine Company, they put the game in a barbershop. They checked the coin box at the end of the first day and found $4. "I figured I had discovered the wheel," Buffett said.[15]

Eventually, the pinball business was netting $50 per week. Later, Buffett bought an unimproved farm in northeastern Nebraska and had $9,000 in the bank by the time he graduated from high school.[16]

~

Buffett developed an early reputation as an investor:

> *"I shorted a few shares of American Telephone because I knew that all my [high school] teachers owned it. They thought I knew about stocks; and I thought if I shorted AT&T, I would terrorize them about their retirement."*[17]

## WORK WHERE YOU WANT TO WORK

When asked why he forgoes working in New York, where he could be nearer the financial markets and the rumor mill, Buffett replied:

> *"With enough inside information and a million dollars, you can go broke in a year."*[18]

~

> *"I probably have more friends in New York and California than here, but this is a good place to bring up children and a good place to live. You can think*

*here. You can think better about the market; you don't hear so many stories, and you can just sit and look at the stock on the desk in front of you. You can think about a lot of things."*[19]

But he also says:

*"If a graduating MBA were to ask me, 'How do I get rich in a hurry?' I would not respond with quotations from Ben Franklin or Horatio Alger but would instead hold my nose with one hand and point with the other toward Wall Street."*[20]

## WORK WITH GOOD PEOPLE

*"I choose to work with every single person that I work with. That ends up being the most important factor. I don't interact with people I don't like or admire. That's the key. It's like marrying."*[21]

~

*"I work with sensational people, and I do what I want in life. Why shouldn't I? If I'm not in a position to do what I want, who the hell is?"*[22]

~

*"Somebody once said that in looking for people to hire, you look for three qualities: integrity, intelligence, and energy. And if they don't have the first, the other two*

*will kill you. You think about it; it's true. If you hire somebody without the first, you really want them to be dumb and lazy."*[23]

When a graduate student sought job counseling, Buffett said:

*"I believe in going to work for businesses you admire and people you admire. Anytime you're around somebody that you're getting something out of and you feel good about the organization, you just have to get a good result. I advise you never to do anything because you think it's miserable now but it's going to be great 10 years from now, or because you think I've got X dollars now, but I'll have 10X. If you're not enjoying it today, you're probably not going to enjoy it 10 years from now."*[24]

Who you work for makes a big difference. Buffett remembers that, at one time, players like Babe Ruth and Lou Gehrig voted a full share of their World Series proceeds to their bat boy:

*"The key in life is to figure out who to be the bat boy for."*[25]

Buffett admits that his advice to college students has had unexpected outcomes:

*"I gave a talk last year; some student at Harvard asked me, 'Who should I go to work for?' I said, "Go to work*

*for whoever you admire the most." I got a call from the dean about two weeks later. He said, 'What are you telling these kids? They're all becoming self-employed.'"*[26]

NOTE: A gentle get-back there? Buffett applied to Harvard before he was admitted to Columbia, but Harvard rejected him. But Buffett seems to hold no grudge. The only brand-new MBA he ever hired was a young woman from Harvard.

## GIVE A PAT ON THE BACK

Buffett wrote to Katharine Graham, late publisher of the *Washington Post,* in 1984:

*"Berkshire Hathaway bought its shares in the* Washington Post *in the spring and summer of 1973. The cost of these shares was $10.6 million, and the present market value is about $140 million. . . . If we had spent this same $10.6 million at the same time in the shares of . . . other [media companies] . . . we now would have either $50 million worth of Dow Jones, $30 million worth of Gannett, $75 million worth of Knight-Ridder, $60 million worth of the* New York Times, *or $40 million of Times Mirror. So, instead of thanks a million, make it thanks anywhere from $65 [million] to $110 million."*[27]

# BE LOYAL TO YOUR PARTNERS

Buffett acknowledges that money and power could give him undue advantage over partners, employees, and others:

> *"One time we had a dog on our roof, and my son called to him and he jumped. He lived, but he broke a leg. It was awful. The dog that loves you so much that he jumps off the roof . . . you can put people into those situations, too. I don't want to do that."*[28]

When Berkshire Hathaway invested in Cap Cities/ ABC, Buffett promised former Chairman Tom Murphy that it would be for the long term, even if the company's television network problems were not quickly resolved:

> *"It's like if you have a kid that has problems: It's not something we're going to sell in five years. We're partners in it."*[29]

~

> *"We're not pure economic creatures, and that policy penalizes our results somewhat; but we prefer to operate that way in life. What's the sense of becoming rich if you're going to have a pattern of operation where you continually discard associations with people you like, admire, and find interesting in order to earn*

*a slightly bigger figure? We like big figures, but not to the exclusion of everything else.*"[30]

~

*"I don't think I would feel good about myself if I went around dumping people after they trusted me."*[31]

NOTE: Cap Cities/ABC was sold to Disney in 1995 for $19 billion. Buffett received Disney shares but later sold them.

~

In the fall of 2005 an unexpected opportunity arose to buy the U.S. operations of British insurer CGNU, PLC, at 70 percent of its book value. The blue light for a bargain was flashing, and Buffett's lifetime practice of making friends and building trust paid off for Berkshire shareholders. Buffett's old friend Jack Byrne, who led a recovery at GEICO, made the sale of Fireman's Fund a success, and gained Buffett's respect in other business deals, took the lead. In partnership with Buffett, Byrne's White Mountains Insurance Group acquired CGNU's U.S. operations, paying $1.7 billion for a unit with a net worth of $3 billion. Buffett contributed $300 million to the deal, and Berkshire ended up owning 30 percent of White Mountains.

Buffett made a quick decision to commit a lot of capital to the deal because he believed in Byrne:

*"Byrne is like the farmer who rolls an ostrich egg into the hen house and says, 'Ladies, this is what the competition is doing.'"*[32]

Jack Byrne retired as chairman and CEO of White Mountains Insurance Group in January 2007.

## GUARD YOUR TIME

Warren's oldest son, Howard, eventually came to understand his father's time management process: "My father couldn't run a lawnmower. . . . I never saw him cut the grass, trim a hedge, or wash a car. I remember that used to be irritating; and only when I got older and understood the value of time did I realize why he did things the way he did. His time is so valuable."[33]

Said Warren Buffett:

*"It's not a plus to get terribly well known. As you can see (waving toward the small suite that makes up Berkshire Hathaway headquarters), we are not equipped to handle tons of inquiries. We get letters from people all over who want advice on investments. I don't like to be hard-nosed, but there's also no way I can do it and get my job done."*[34]

Buffett rarely gives speeches or makes public appearances on behalf of civic or business organizations. But he does make about a dozen speeches, mostly question-and-answer sessions, at universities each year.

> *"If you talk to 100 students and you say something that makes sense, a few of them may pay attention to it, and it may actually change their lives, as opposed to a bunch of 60-year-olds."*

Buffett, who was 63 when he said this, apparently knew it from experience.

> *"I mean, I can go hear a speech and I know whether I'm entertained or not, but I probably won't change anything I do."*[35]

Buffett can be generous with his time and assets: He once donated a lunch date to a foundation supporting San Francisco's Glide Memorial Church's work with the homeless. The Glide Foundation auctioned the lunch off on eBay for $620,100. But Buffett also defends his boundaries. When Buffett planned to replace his 2001 Lincoln Town Car, he donated it to Girls Inc., where Suzie Jr. serves on the board of directors. The car had a *Kelly Blue Book* value of $11,200. Bill Zanker, founder of The Learning Annex, bought the car for $73,200. He announced that he would go to Omaha to take delivery and, at that time, hold a news conference with Buffett. Zanker got the car but not Buffett.

"I timed it wrong," explained Zanker. "I should have called his office first."

It also was no-go when Zanker offered to donate $2 million to charity if Buffett would speak for 30 minutes to one of The Learning Annex real estate and wealth seminars. Buffett politely explained that he preferred to teach adults at Berkshire's annual meeting.[36]

Buffett borrowed his time-management principles from a pro:

*"Well, I just use the Nancy Reagan policy. I just say no."*[37]

## KNOW WHEN TO QUIT

*"That which is not worth doing is not worth doing well."*[38]

~

*"If at first you do succeed, quit trying."*[39]

In 1969, when the stock market was on a high, Buffett took early retirement. He shut down the Buffett Partnership, which had experienced a thirtyfold increase in value, and returned the money to investors. He was 38 years old:

*"I don't want to be totally occupied with outpacing an investment rabbit all my life."*

He added:

*"I have no urge to keep piling up money."*

And finally:

*"The only way to slow down is to stop."*[40]

NOTE: He didn't stay away from work long. Buffett was soon creating his new investment vehicle, Berkshire Hathaway, from the cloth of a textile manufacturing concern.

# — About Running — a Business

## COMMUNICATE WELL

How does Buffett write such clear and candid annual reports, especially since they have no graphs or photos? He writes as if for someone he knows.

*"I just assume my sister owns the other half of the business and she's been traveling for a year. She's not business-ignorant, but she's not an expert either. I don't see anything wrong with graphics. It's just that I think there is a tendency when people emphasize, to deemphasize real information."*[1]

~

*"If you understand an idea, you can express it so others can understand it. I find that every year when*

*I write the report, I hit these blocks. The block isn't because I've run out of words in the dictionary. The block is because I haven't got it straight in my own mind yet. There's nothing like writing to force you to think and to get your thoughts straight."*[2]

Berkshire's high share price is one way of communicating to people that Buffett wants serious investors who acquire the shares for the long term. He wants people to know what they're getting into:

*"We could stick a sign outside this hall tonight and put 'rock concert' on it, and we'd have one kind of crowd come in. And we could put 'ballet,' and we'd have a somewhat different kind of crowd come in. Both crowds are fine. But it's a terrible mistake to put rock concert out there if you're going to have a ballet, or vice versa. And the only way I have of sticking a sign on Berkshire, as to the kind of place I'm asking people to enter, is through the communications and policies."*[3]

## KNOW WHEN TO SAY NO

When asked to comment on the 1992 purchase of shares in Wells Fargo & Co., a woman answering the telephone at Berkshire gave the company's standard reply: "It has long been the policy at Berkshire Hathaway that we never comment on our portfolio or rumors about our portfolio."[4]

There is a reason for Buffett's silence on investment activities:

*"If I say anything, I know it [the low price that interests him] will be gone. You can't telegraph your punches in a financial situation."* [5]

When Buffett wants to send a warning shot across the bow, he is capable of expressing himself succinctly. Such was the case when he worked with Salomon to resolve its government securities trading improprieties:

*"We [Salomon] will pay any fines or penalties with dispatch, and we will also try to settle valid legal claims promptly. However, we will litigate invalid or inflated claims, of which there will be many, to whatever extent necessary. That is, we will make appropriate amends for past conduct, but we will be no one's patsy."* [6]

NOTE: For more on the Salomon scandal, go to page 108.

## SET AN EXAMPLE

During his stint as interim chairman of Salomon Inc., Buffett told shareholders:

*"An atmosphere encouraging exemplary behavior is probably even more important than rules, necessary though they are. During my tenure as chairman, I will*

*consider myself the firm's chief compliance officer, and I have asked all 9,000 of Salomon's employees to assist me in that effort. I have also urged them to be guided by a test that goes beyond rules. Contemplating any business act, an employee should ask himself whether he would be willing to see it immediately described by an informed and critical reporter on the front page of his local paper, there to be read by his spouse, children, and friends. At Salomon, we simply want no part of any activities that pass legal tests but that we, as citizens, would find offensive."*[7]

## THE BERKSHIRE HATHAWAY ANNUAL MEETING

Many thousands of investors and admirers descend upon Omaha each spring to sit in a crowded meeting hall for hours to hear what Warren Buffett has to say. He stays until all questions are answered; and if the questions are still rolling in when lunchtime comes, shareholders can go to the lobby to buy sandwiches and a Coca-Cola. Every year, Buffett sets down the rules by which the annual meeting will be conducted. These examples are collected from several different years:

*"The business of the meeting will be handled in our usual Stalinistic manner to allow plenty of time to answer shareholder's questions."*[8]

*"If you must leave during the meeting, it's better form to leave while Charlie's talking—which is rarely."*[9]

~

*"We'll be here to answer questions until around noon or until Charlie says something optimistic, whichever comes first."*[10]

~

*"After the meeting, there will be buses to take out-of-town guests to the Nebraska Furniture Mart, Borsheim's jewelry, or anyplace else that Berkshire has an economic interest in."*[11]

The preceding is no joke. In the lobby of the meeting hall, there are carts selling See's Candy, Ginzu knives, *World Book* encyclopedias, cowboy boots, modular homes, and other Berkshire Hathaway–owned products. The trips to the Berkshire Hathaway–owned stores not only allow people to shop, but also serve an educational purpose, Buffett insists. One must, he used to say, "go to the Nebraska Furniture Mart and see Mrs. B in her natural setting."[12]

Charlie Munger occasionally makes a marketing pitch of his own. He especially likes the *World Book* encyclopedia: "I give away more of that product than any other product that Berkshire Hathaway makes. . . . It's a perfectly fabulous human achievement. To edit something that user friendly with that much wisdom encapsulated is a fabulous thing."[15]

As more people become Berkshire shareholders, logistics for the annual meeting get trickier:

> *"Most of you know we held our annual meeting at the Joslyn Art Museum the past several years until we outgrew it. Since the Orpheum Theater, where we're meeting today, is an old vaudeville theater, I suppose we've slid down the cultural chain. Don't ask me where we'll go next."*[14]

In 1995, the meeting moved to the convention center at the Holiday Inn; and again, the hall was packed. Berkshire's shareholder base doubled in 1996 with the issuance of the Berkshire B shares. The meeting next moved to Aksarben Fairgrounds. Omaha then built a new state-of-the-art convention center, the Qwest Center. In 2007, more than 20,000 people showed up, filling the Qwest Center to capacity.

## TAKE CARE OF SHAREHOLDERS

Berkshire Hathaway investor Gerald L. "Bud" Pearson says he heard about Buffett from a friend in 1965. Pearson went to talk to Buffett, who told him that he'd stopped accepting new investors to his partnership. After talking to Pearson for an hour, Buffett changed his mind.

"Aw, heck, you seem like a nice guy," Buffett said. In time, Pearson became a "Buffett millionaire."[15]

~

The board of directors at Berkshire are inspired to take care of shareholders for more than one reason. First of all, the board member are shareholders, and most hold considerable shares. Also, Berkshire does not carry directors' and officers' liability insurance. If the board is sued for misconduct, it could cost them a considerable amount of money.

~

When asked why thousands of shareholders travel long distances to attend Berkshire Hathaway's annual meeting in Omaha each year, Buffett surmised:

*"They come because we make them feel like owners."*[16]

~

Buffett likes to invest in businesses where managers think like owners. He tried to shift the corporate culture at Salomon:

*"We wish to see the unit's managers become wealthy* through *ownership, not by simply free-riding on the ownership of others. I think, in fact, that ownership can in time bring our best managers substantial wealth, perhaps in amounts well beyond what they now think possible."*[17]

# GOODBYE TO A GOOD IDEA

Charlie Munger, in 1981, questioned why corporate leaders should decide what charities their shareholders support. After all, the money that companies distribute actually belongs to shareholders. So that year, he and Buffett instituted a giving program that allowed each shareholder to designate up to three charities; donations would be sent to those charities in proportion to the number of A shares held by the shareholder. When B shares were later issued, their holders could not participate.

The idea caught on quickly. In the 22 years it operated, Berkshire's shareholder giving program distributed $197 million to about 3,500 charities. The overwhelming favorite recipients were schools, churches, and synagogues. Buffett and Munger gave their portion to their charitable trusts, which traditionally supported—among other things—family planning efforts.

The Berkshire giving model was widely admired by policy makers, even conservative ones. Nobel laureate economist Milton Freidman noted that the democratic process was subverted when corporations gave away shareholder's money to charities without consulting them. Representative Paul Gillmor (R-OH) in 1997 even tried to pass legislation requiring all corporations to adopt the Berkshire model.

Yet from the outset, a small group opposed the plan, mainly because some of the money went to so-called liberal causes, especially to reproductive rights. An antiabortion group called Life Decisions International organized an unsuccessful consumer boycott against Berkshire subsidiaries and, in 2002, submitted a shareholders' resolution to end Berkshire's giving program. The resolution was defeated by 97 percent of shareholders.

Then in 2002, Berkshire acquired Pampered Chef, the nation's largest kitchenware company, from its founder, Doris K. Christopher. Pampered Chef is a direct seller of cookwares through individual distributors who usually sell at private parties in homes. Pampered Chef became a target for the boycott, and sales took a dive as sales associates and their customers abandoned the company to avoid involvement in the program. Buffett and Munger saw Christopher's company and Berkshire's investment slipping away. They decided to wrap up the precedent-setting corporate gift program, even though Munger admitted, "It killed me."[18]

Munger needn't have been too sad. There are hundreds of investors who became multimillionaires, even billionaires, through their early Berkshire investments. The company's charitable giving program wasn't the only way they share the wealth. Many of these multigenerational investors have charitable foundations or organizations of their own choosing that return to society some of the benefits they have received. Donald and Mildred Topp Othmer each invested $25,000 in the Buffett Partnership in the early 1960s. When Donald, a chemical engineering professor, died in 1995, his estate held approximately 7,000 shares, which went to charity. When Mildred died in 1998, she left $750 million to charity. Even though a niece challenged—and a court modified—Mildred's will, charities still benefited hugely. For example, Buffett's alma mater, the University of Nebraska, received $125 million.

## THE SALOMON SCANDAL

Salomon bond trader Paul Mozer was charged with illegal trading of U.S. Treasury bonds, allegedly in an attempt to corner the market. The incident posed a serious threat to the survival of the entire company. Buffett observed:

*"Mozer's paying $30,000 and is sentenced to prison for four months. Salomon's shareholders—including me—paid $290 million, and I got sentenced to ten months as CEO."*[19]

While serving as interim chairman, Buffett presided over the 1992 Salomon Brothers annual meeting. It lasted three hours, as Buffett faced a grilling from shareholders who wanted more information about Salomon's government bond-trading offenses. Berkshire Hathaway held a major investment in Salomon, and Buffett was working without salary to restore the company's credibility in the market after Mozer's crime. Famous gadfly shareholder Evelyn Y. Davis asked Buffett how he could justify charging $158,000 for the cost of his corporate jet, which shuttled Buffett between Omaha and New York City. Buffett answered:

*"I work cheap, but I travel expensive."*[20]

Davis also groused about the $25 million in lawyer's fees associated with the resolution of Salomon's problems, to which Buffett replied:

*"I would be delighted to have you negotiate with them, Evelyn. And I think the mere mention of that would be enough to induce a little moderation."*[21]

NOTE: Travelers bought Salomon in 1997, then it was merged into Citicorp in 1998. Berkshire has no position in the company now.

## BERKSHIRE HATHAWAY ONLINE

Buffett has called his shareholders a community. They are residents of a fictional global village called Graham & Doddsville, named after Ben Graham and David Dodd, the legendary fathers of the value investing philosophy. Residents of Graham & Doddsville gather for their annual reunion the first weekend in May in Omaha, and now they convene in cyberspace. Buffett announced in the 1996 annual report that although "it was a close decision," he and Munger decided to put the annual report on the Internet. They would always post the report on Saturdays so that readers would have time to digest the news before trading opened Monday morning. Berkshire's website, www .berkshirehathaway.com, now has more than reports. It provides pitches for GEICO, news releases, comments by Buffett, and the purest facts and figures on the company. There also are numerous blogs and message boards, such as one at Ragingbull@lycos.com. Perhaps the most popular is found at messageboards@aol.com. Occasionally, you'll find a posting from Suzie Jr., using the name Doshoes.

## HIRE WELL, MANAGE LITTLE

Author Robert Miles says Buffett is not only a value investor, he is also a "value manager." He's always seeking great managers.[22]

Buffett says his employment form has one question:

*"Are you a fanatic?"*

The best managers are.[23]

*"I like guys who forget that they sold the business to me and run the show like proprietors. When I marry the daughter, she continues to live with her parents."*[24]

Buffett expects his managers to be that way:

*"If they need my help to manage the enterprise, we're probably both in trouble."*[25]

There are exceptions to that policy. Each year, Buffett sets prices on See's Candy and circulation rates for the *Buffalo News*. Both management and Buffett say that because he's some distance from the operations, he has greater objectivity.

## PUT A PREMIUM ON EXPERIENCE

There is no retirement age at Berkshire Hathaway. The CEOs there serve an average of 23 years:

> *"Can you really explain to a fish what it's like to walk on land? One day on land is worth a thousand years of talking about it, and one day running a business has exactly the same kind of value."*[26]

~

> *"In a general sense, gray hair doesn't hurt on this playing field: You don't need good hand-eye coordination or well-toned muscles to push money around (thank heavens). As long as our minds continue to function effectively, Charlie and I can keep on doing our jobs pretty much as we have in the past."*[27]

## BE SMART ABOUT ALLOCATING CAPITAL

An advantage of owning a company outright, rather than simply holding shares, is the ability to reinvest profits efficiently, even if that means moving funds to a different industry:

> *"We're not in the steel business, per se. We're not in the shoe business, per se. We're not in any business, per se. We're big in insurance, but we're not committed to it. We don't have a mind-set that says you have to go down this road. So we can take capital and move it into businesses that make sense."*[28]

## BE BRAVE

After he finished college, Buffett invested $100 in a Dale Carnegie course:

> *". . . not to prevent my knees from knocking when public speaking but to do public speaking while my knees were knocking."*[29]

## USE CROSSOVER SKILLS

> *"I am a better investor because I am a businessman and a better businessman because I am an investor."*[30]

~

> *"I feel the same way about managing that I do about investing: It's just not necessary to do extraordinary things to get extraordinary results."*[31]

# THE MIGHTY MACHINE CALLED BERKSHIRE HATHAWAY

For many years, if you said the name Berkshire Hathaway Corporation, people asked, "Don't they make shirts?" No, and the company never has. When Warren Buffett started buying shares, Berkshire was a declining New England textile mill. Buffett has called it one of his biggest investment mistakes. After trying and trying to rescue the mill, Buffett finally shut it down. But he didn't give up the corporate shell that remained. Instead, he slowly and deliberately transformed it into the greatest holding company anywhere, ever. The company has 217,000 employees and annual revenues of nearly $100 billion.

But the company has another distinguishing aspect—some people see Berkshire as a cult with the Oracle of Omaha the cult leader. If this were the case, belonging to this cult has been profitable.

If you had invested $10,000 in Berkshire in 1965, your investment would have been worth more than $30 million by 2006. If you had put that same money in the Standard & Poor's (S&P) 500 stock index and left it there, you'd have a measly $500,000. Morningstar reports that since 1965, Berkshire's book value per share has grown at nearly 22 percent per year. Over the same time, the S&P grew by 10.4 percent.

Berkshire is the parent to more than 65 companies and owns around 39 different stocks. It holds positions in a variety of industries, from furniture to fast food to footwear to underwear. Most of its assets, however, are in insurance companies. GEICO is the fourth-largest auto insurer in the United States. General Re Corporation and Berkshire Reinsurance Group are two of the largest reinsurers in the world. General Re is the world's only AAA-rated reinsurance company. (Insurance companies buy reinsurance to help offset major risks, especially unpredictable ones, such as hurricanes and earthquakes.)

Buffett built Berkshire into one of the eight companies with a Moody's Aaa rating, the highest credit rating achievable. How did he do it? Buffett began by focusing on stocks and gradually started buying entire businesses at favorable prices. He then kept debt at a minimum and allocated capital back into the businesses in ways that boosted profitability.

One of the most impressive Berkshire assets is its cash holdings: In 2006, Berkshire had $42 billion in reserves. Former Paine Webber analyst Alice Schroeder says, "Berkshire is now clearly an insurance company that will generate excess capital and cash flow that can be invested; and, of course, the real synergy here is that Warren Buffett is the master at allocating and using capital."[32]

Even with the heavy weighting of insurance companies, Buffett says:

> *"The company has a multitude of diversified and powerful streams of earnings, Gibraltar-like financial strength, and a deeply imbedded culture of acting in the best interest of shareholders. Outstanding managers are available to succeed me. I expect Berkshire to become ever-stronger and more profitable as it makes new acquisitions and expands present businesses."*[33]

While Berkshire may not precisely fit the description of a cult, it certainly has become a community of true believers. Investors tend to buy and then refuse to sell, even instructing their heirs to hold on. The annual meeting is sometimes called a hajj, and Buffett himself dubbed it the Woodstock for investors. Fortunately, Buffett is far too practical to ask shareholders to drink Kool-Aid or to follow him over a cliff. But he does expect them to hold on during times when the stock isn't skyrocketing and to boldly shop at all Berkshire subsidiaries. And they do.

# — About Investing —

Warren Buffett employs investment principles that he describes as "simple, old, and few."[1] Many of Buffett's methods evolve from his personality and character. Others he has learned from teachers and experience. Like all good students, he uses his training as a foundation. In time, he stacked the bricks far higher than his best teachers.

## HAVE A PHILOSOPHY

*"Rule No. 1: Never lose money. Rule No. 2: Never forget Rule No. 1."*[2]

~

*"Over the years, a number of very smart people have learned the hard way that a long stream of impressive numbers multiplied by a single zero always equals zero."*[3]

Buffett returns again and again to Ben Graham:

> *"I consider there to be three basic ideas, ideas that if they are really ground into your intellectual framework, I don't see how you could help but do reasonably well in stocks. None of them are complicated. None of them take mathematical talent or anything of the sort. [Graham] said you should look at stocks as small pieces of the business. Look at [market] fluctuations as your friend rather than your enemy—profit from folly rather than participate in it. And in [the last chapter of* The Intelligent Investor*], he said the three most important words of investing: 'margin of safety.' I think those ideas, 100 years from now, will still be regarded as the three cornerstones of sound investing."*[4]

Buffett summarizes Graham this way:

> *"When proper temperament joins with proper intellectual framework, then you get rational behavior."*[5]

Buffett is not concerned about his principles going stale:

> *"If principles can become dated, they're not principles."*[6]

## RECOGNIZE THE ENEMY: INFLATION

> *"The arithmetic makes it plain that inflation is a far more devastating tax than anything that has been enacted by our legislature. The inflation tax has a fantastic ability*

*to simply consume capital. It makes no difference to a widow with her savings in a 5 percent passbook account whether she pays 100 percent income tax on her interest income during a period of zero inflation or pays no income taxes during years of 5 percent inflation. Either way, she is 'taxed' in a manner that leaves her no real income whatsoever. Any money she spends comes right out of capital. She would find outrageous a 120 percent income tax but doesn't seem to notice that 5 percent inflation is the economic equivalent."[7]*

~

*"If you feel you can dance in and out of securities in a way that defeats the inflation tax, I would like to be your broker—but not your partner."[8]*

Buffett explains why he holds stocks even in times of high inflation:

*"Partly, it's habit. Partly, it's just that stocks mean business, and owning businesses is much more interesting than owning gold or farmland. Besides, stocks are probably still the best of all the poor alternatives in an era of inflation—at least they are if you buy in at appropriate prices."[9]*

Buffett has a few ideas on how to control inflation:

*"I could eliminate inflation or reduce it very easily if you had a constitutional amendment that said that no*

*congressman or senator was eligible for reelection in a year in which the CPI increased more than over 3 percent."*[10]

## EXPERIENCE EPIPHANY

Buffett was 19 years old and a senior at the University of Nebraska when he read Graham's classic *The Intelligent Investor*. He likens the experience to that of "Paul on the road to Damascus" and one in which he learned the philosophy of "buying $1 for 40 cents."[11] Buffett says that before reading the book:

*"I went the whole gamut. I collected charts and I read all the technical stuff. I listened to tips. And then I picked up Graham's* The Intelligent Investor. *That was like seeing the light."*[12]

~

*"I don't want to sound like a religious fanatic or anything, but it really did get me."*[13]

~

*"Prior to that, I had been investing with my glands instead of my head."*[14]

# BENJAMIN GRAHAM

Warren Buffett first became acquainted with Graham when he read his book *The Intelligent Investor*. He met his hero in person in 1950 when Buffett enrolled in graduate school at Columbia University: "Next to my dad, Ben Graham had more impact certainly on my business life than any individual," Buffett says.[15]

Graham, he explained, was more interested in the intellectual challenge of investing than in building a fortune. That, along with vast intellectual curiosity, generosity, and a wry sense of humor, made Graham unique.[16]

~

Graham and Buffett had much in common. Articulate and witty, Graham enjoyed a wide circle of friends. The chief similarity is a peculiar (to the rest of us) disinterest in lots of money. Shortly after Buffett joined Graham's firm, Graham told him: "Money won't make any difference to you and me. We won't change. Only our wives will live better."[17]

When Buffett graduated from Columbia in 1951, Graham suggested that he postpone his career in investments until the overheated market took a rest. During that year, the Dow Jones Industrial Average hit 250. Until then, the DJIA had traded at below 200 in every year since its inception.

"I had about 10 thousand bucks," Buffett said. "If I'd taken [the] advice, I'd probably still have about 10 thousand bucks."[18]

It was an uncharacteristic suggestion, since Graham had built a career warning against market timing. Graham retired in 1956, apparently weary of working and no longer interested in stocks.

NOTE: Buffett ended up with much more money than Graham. When Graham died in 1976 at age 82, he left an estate of around $3 million.

*"[Graham] wasn't about brilliant investments and he wasn't about fads or fashion. He was about sound investing, and I think sound investing can make you very wealthy if you're not in too big of a hurry. And it never makes you poor, which is better."*[19]

~

*"It baffles us how many people know of Ben Graham, but so few follow. We tell our principles freely and write about them extensively in our annual reports. They are easy to learn. They should be easy to follow. But the only thing anyone wants to know is, 'What are you buying today?' Like Graham, we are widely recognized but least followed."*[20]

~

*"Most of us, when we get our ideas about investing, we guard them jealously and don't talk about them until we've bought the last share that we can afford. Then we start shouting. Ben was something else on that. He*

*regularly taught at Columbia or the New York Institute of Finance. He never taught a class without current examples, and he was perfectly willing to share what other people thought of as secrets. It is sort of the ultimate act of generosity when you go out and teach someone something that is actually going to be harmful to your own commercial well-being, and I saw Ben do that.*[21]

Buffett laughed and added, "That is a part of Ben I didn't carry forward."

NOTE: Buffett does not reveal his purchases until required to do so by the Securities and Exchange Commission or long after the fact when explaining Berkshire Hathaway's performance to investors. Generally, Berkshire does not announce investments of under $600 million.

Here are some typical Graham observations on investing and the markets:

*"Pascal said that 'the heart has reasons that reason doesn't understand.' For 'heart,' read 'Wall Street.'"*[22]

Though Graham, like Buffett, had an innate love for math, he warned against any investor who bases investments on overly impressive charts, graphs, or formulas:

*"Even when the underlying motive of a purchaser of a security is mere speculative greed, human nature desires to conceal this unlovely impulse behind a screen of apparent logic and good sense."*[23]

Graham often reminded investors that they own the companies in which they invest and, as owners, should not let themselves be bullied by management:

> *"I want to say a word about disgruntled shareholders. In my humble opinion, not enough of them are disgruntled. And one of the great troubles with Wall Street is that it cannot distinguish between a mere troublemaker or 'strike suitor' in corporate affairs and a stockholder with a legitimate complaint which deserves attention from his management and from his shareholders."*[24]

Despite his admiration for Graham, Buffett departs from him in several notable ways:

> *"Ben Graham wanted everything to be a quantitative bargain. I want it to be a quantitative bargain in terms of future streams of cash. My guess is the last big time to do it Ben's way was in '73 or '74, when you could have done it quite easily."*[25]

~

> *"I'm willing to pay more for a good business and for good management than I would 20 years ago. Ben tended to look at the statistics alone. I've looked more and more at the intangibles."*[26]

~

The late William Ruane, founder of the highly successful Sequoia Fund, met Warren Buffett when both attended

Graham's seminar at Columbia. Together, Ruane said, Graham and Buffett paint a complete picture of how to invest:

*"[Graham] wrote what we call the Bible, and Warren's thinking updated it. Warren wrote the New Testament."*[27]

~

In his later years, Graham told Buffett that every day he hoped to do "something foolish, something creative, and something generous." Graham said he usually was able to get the first one accomplished before breakfast.[28]

When Graham was in his late seventies and lay ill in a San Diego hospital, he asked Buffett to help him revise *The Intelligent Investor* for a new edition. Buffett agreed, but later Graham recovered and proceeded on his own. Graham seemed not to like the modifications Buffett proposed. What were those changes? Not many, Buffett said:

*"I wanted to talk a little more about inflation and about how the investor should analyze businesses. But I was not going to change the ten commandments at all."*[29]

~

For several decades, Graham's theories have seldom been included in college curriculums because, according to Buffett:

*"It's not difficult enough. So, instead, something is taught that is difficult but not useful. The business schools reward complex behavior more than simple behavior, but simple behavior is more effective."*[30]

However, after Buffett's fame and success spread, Columbia, Stanford, and other business schools included Graham's teachings in their coursework.

Buffett now hears from investors all over the world who share his admiration for Benjamin Graham: "He was true north on a lot of people's compass," Buffett says.[31]

What did Graham have to say about Buffett? Graham told Del Mar, California, investor Charles Brandes, "Warren has done very well." [32]

# NEVER MIND WHAT THE PROFESSORS SAY

Buffett rails against investment theories such as efficient market hypothesis, beta, and other concepts taught today at the major universities. They rely, he believes, too heavily on abstract theory and not enough on common sense:

*"I'd be a bum on the street with a tin cup if the markets were always efficient."*[33]

~

*"Investing in a market where people believe in efficiency is like playing bridge with someone who has been told it doesn't do any good to look at the cards."*[34]

~

*"It has been helpful to me to have tens of thousands [of students] turned out of business schools taught that it didn't do any good to think."*[35]

~

*"Current finance classes can help you do average."*[36]

Buffett's partner, Charlie Munger, when asked about modern portfolio theory, instantly replied, "Twaddle!" He added that the concepts are "a type of dementia I can't even classify."[37]

As for "asset allocation" to the future highest and best-performing industrial group, Buffett also passes:

*"For me, it's what's available at the time. We're not interested in categories per se. We're interested in value."*[38]

## MEET MR. MARKET—YOUR SERVANT, NOT YOUR GUIDE

"Mr. Market" was a character invented by Ben Graham to illuminate his students' minds regarding market behavior. The stock market should be viewed as an emotionally disturbed business partner, Graham said.[39] This partner, Mr. Market, shows up each day offering a price at which he will buy your share of the business or sell you his share. No matter how wild his offer is or how often you reject it, Mr. Market returns with a new offer the next day and each day thereafter. Buffett says the moral of the story is this: Mr. Market is your servant, not your guide.

In March 1989, as the stock market soared, Buffett wrote:

*"We have no idea how long the excesses will last, nor do we know what will change the attitudes of the government, lender, and buyer that fuel them. But we know that the less prudence with which others conduct their affairs, the greater the prudence with which we should conduct our own affairs."*[40]

In the last years of the twentieth century, Berkshire's price nose-dived, kicked off the diving board by investors' irrational exuberance over anything technology or Internet related, problems with the General Re acquisition, rumors of Buffett's ill health and his inability to live up to his past brilliance. In mid-1998, Berkshire was selling at a high of $80,000; by March 2000, it was selling for almost half that much. Buffett wrote in the 2001 annual report:

*"Here's one for those who enjoy an odd coincidence: The Great Bubble ended on March 10, 2000 (though we didn't realize that fact until some months later). On that day, the NASDAQ (recently 1,731) hit its all-time high of 5,132. That same day, Berkshire shares traded at $40,800, their lowest price since mid-1997."*[41]

Nevertheless, during the dark days, Berkshire's book value increased, albeit by a small amount. And by 2005, Berkshire's share price had more than recovered. Buffett, however, lamented that he had not captured more profits when some of his permanent holdings were wildly overpriced.

*"I made a big mistake in not selling several of our larger holdings during the Great Bubble. If these stocks are fully priced now, you must wonder what I was thinking four years ago when their intrinsic value was lower and their prices far higher. So do I."*[42]

When conditions are reversed, how can an investor be sure that a stock that is undervalued by the market eventually will rise?

*"When I worked for Graham-Newman, I asked Ben Graham, who then was my boss, about that. He just shrugged and replied that the market always eventually does. He was right: In the short run, [the market is] a voting machine; in the long run, it's a weighing machine."*[43]

~

*"The fact that people will be full of greed, fear, or folly is predictable. The sequence is not predictable."*[44]

~

*"The market, like the Lord, helps those who help themselves."*[45]

# IGNORE MR. MARKET'S MOODS

*"Charlie and I never have an opinion on the market because it wouldn't be any good and it might interfere with the opinions we have that are good."*[46]

~

*"You can't get rich with a weather vane."*[47]

~

*"The market is there only as a reference point to see if anybody is offering to do anything foolish. When we invest in stocks, we invest in businesses."*[48]

~

*"If we find a company we like, the level of the market will not really impact our decisions. We will decide company by company. We spend essentially no time thinking about macroeconomic factors. In other words, if somebody handed us a prediction by the most revered intellectual on the subject, with figures for unemployment or interest rates or whatever it might be for the next two years, we would not pay any attention to it. We simply try to focus on businesses that we think we understand and where we like the price and management. If we see anything that relates to what's going to happen in Congress, we don't even read it. We just don't think it's helpful to have a view on these matters."*[49]

~

*"[John Maynard] Keynes essentially said, Don't try to figure out what the market is doing. Figure out a business you understand, and concentrate."*[50]

~

*"For some reason, people take their cues from price action rather than from values. What doesn't work is when you start doing things that you don't understand or because they worked last week for somebody else. The dumbest reason in the world to buy a stock is because it's going up."*[51]

~

*"The future is never clear; you pay a very high price in the stock market for a cheery consensus. Uncertainty actually is the friend of the buyer of long-term values."*[52]

## LISTEN FOR OPPORTUNITY'S CALL

Though Buffett cannot anticipate market movements, there are times when it is obvious that stock prices in general are too high or too low. The clue is that there are either very few undervalued stocks to buy (the market is in the stratosphere) or there are so many good buys that an investor can't take advantage of them all (the market is bottoming). In 1973, stocks were high priced.

*"I felt like an oversexed guy on a desert island. I [didn't] find anything to buy."*[53]

In 1974, Buffett's condition didn't change, but his location (like the market) did. He told a reporter:

*"I feel like an oversexed guy in a harem. This is the time to start investing."*[54]

~

*"Overall, Berkshire and its long-term shareholders benefit from a sinking stock market much as a regular purchaser of food benefits from declining food prices. So when the market plummets—as it will from time to time—neither panic nor mourn. It's good news for Berkshire."*[55]

At times, Buffett finds no attractive investments:

*"Currently liking neither stocks nor bonds, I find myself the polar opposite of Mae West as she declared, 'I only like two kinds of men: foreign and domestic.'"*[56]

Buffett says he likes to buy stocks when the "bears are giving them away."[57]

Whether market conditions seem auspicious or not, opportunities can just appear. One occurred when a group of students from the University of Tennessee made the school's annual field trip to Omaha to study Berkshire Hathaway and to meet with Buffett. Each year, at the end of the sessions, the students present him with a gift, such a football signed by their coach, a basketball, or the like. In 2003, they gave Buffett a book, the autobiography of Jim Clayton, founder of Clayton Homes.

*"I already knew the company to be a class act of the manufactured housing industry, knowledge I acquired after earlier making the mistake of buying some distressed junk debt of Oakwood Homes, one of the industry's largest companies. At the time of that purchase, I did not understand how atrocious consumer-financing practices had become throughout the manufactured housing industry. But I learned: Oakwood rather promptly went bankrupt."*[58]

Buffett knew Clayton "behaved considerably better than its major competitors" in lending. On receiving the book, Buffett told the students how much he admired Clayton; and soon afterward, he called Kevin Clayton, Jim's son, to say so. In that telephone call, Buffett became convinced that Kevin, who now runs the company, had two supreme managerial traits—he was both honest and competent.

*"Soon thereafter, I made an offer for the business based solely on Jim's book, my evaluation of Kevin, the public financials of Clayton, and what I had learned from the Oakwood experience."*[59]

Clayton's board jumped at the offer, since difficulties in the industry in general made large-scale financing difficult. They were glad to let Buffett provide and manage capital while they operated the company. Then the story came full circle: Clayton bought the assets of Oakwood.

*"When the transaction closes, Clayton's manufacturing capacity, geographical reach, and sales outlets will be substantially increased. As a by-product, the debt of Oakwood that we own, which we bought at a deep discount, will probably return a small profit to us."*[60]

# KNOW THE DIFFERENCE BETWEEN PRICE AND VALUE

*"Price is what you pay. Value is what you get."*[61]

~

When Berkshire acquired Central States Indemnity Co. of Omaha in 1992, William M. Kizer Sr. described the negotiations this way: "The price he quoted us was that he buys companies for 10 times [annual] earnings. I suggested, 'Well, last year we made $10 million, so if my multiplication is right, that's $100 million,' and I gulped. And he said, 'Okay.' And I said, '$125 million?' He said, 'You're too late.'"[62]

# SEEK INTRINSIC VALUE

Intrinsic value is a critical and at the same time an elusive concept:

*"There is no formula to figure [intrinsic value] out. You have to know the business [whose stock you are considering buying]."*[63]

~

*"Valuing a business is part art and part science."*[64]

~

*"It doesn't have to be rock bottom to buy it. It has to be selling for less than you think the value of the business is, and it has to be run by honest and able people. But if you can buy into a business for less than it's worth today, and you're confident of the management, and you buy into a group of businesses like that, you're going to make money."*[65]

Don't worry about value investors snapping up all the bargains:

*"I have seen no trend toward value investing in the 35 years I've practiced it. There seems to be some perverse human characteristic that likes to make easy things difficult."*[66]

## EXPECT TO BE OUT OF STEP

*"Berkshire buys when the lemmings are heading the other way."*[67]

~

*"Most people get interested in stocks when everyone else is. The time to get interested is when no one else is. You can't buy what is popular and do well."*[68]

~

*"You don't need to be a rocket scientist. Investing is not a game where the guy with the 160 IQ beats the guy with a 130 IQ. Rationality is essential."*[69]

~

*"Happily, there's more than one way to get to financial heaven."*[70]

## THE USED-CIGAR-BUTT SCHOOL OF INVESTING

### A GENTLE DISCOURSE BETWEEN WALTER SCHLOSS AND WARREN BUFFETT

A zealous student of Ben Graham at Columbia, Warren Buffett went to New Jersey for an annual meeting of a company in which Graham owned shares. Walter Schloss, who worked at Graham-Newman Co., also was there. They struck up a conversation, went to lunch, and have been friends ever since. Schloss later left the Graham firm and went into business for himself. Buffett spotlighted Schloss's remarkable investment record in his now famous essay, "The Super Investors of Graham and Doddsville."

Through 39 years, thick and thin, Schloss has delivered a compound annual gain of just over 20 percent, compared to a Standard & Poor's (S&P) Industrials advance of just under 10 percent. Schloss keeps fund expenses at a minimum and forgoes management fees in years his funds make no gains. "I don't think I should get paid if I do a lousy job," Schloss says.[71]

"I think Walter's operational style should be a lesson for us all (one Charlie has already mastered). In effect, Walter is running an office for a year on what it costs Berkshire to start the engines on The Indefensible," Buffett said.[72]

The following is a condensed version of affectionate bantering between Buffett and Schloss[73] at Benjamin Graham's 100th birthday memorial at the New York Society of Security Analysts. Buffett explained that Graham felt it was sort of cheating to use any tool, such as meetings with top management, that are not available to individual investors.

*Buffett:* I was inclined to cheat, but Walter has been more of a purist on that. Over the years, he's got some investment record, I'll tell you that!

*Schloss:* I really don't like talking to management. Stocks really are easier to deal with. They don't argue with you. They don't have emotional problems. You don't have to hold their hand. Now, Warren is an unusual guy because he's not only a good analyst, he's a good salesman, and he's a very good judge of people. That's an unusual combination. If I were to [acquire] somebody with a business, I'm sure he would quit the very next day. I would misjudge his character or something—or I wouldn't understand that he really didn't like the business and really wanted to sell it and get out. Warren's people knock themselves out after he buys the business, so that's an unusual trait.

*Schloss (later in the discussion):* I own a lot of stocks. Warren doesn't *like* that, but I can't *help* it. You have to do what's comfortable for you, even if it's not as profitable as what Warren does. There's only one Warren. [Because I own so many stocks], the risk of any one is not that great. I try to buy securities that are undervalued based on assets more than earnings. I do a better job on assets than earnings because earnings have a way of changing.

*Buffett (later in the conversation, not ready to give up on this):* Walter has owned hundreds and hundreds and hundreds of securities. I call it the used-cigar-butt approach. You find these well-smoked, down-to-the-nub cigars; but they're free. You pick them up and get one free puff out of them. Anything is a buy at a price. Lately, Walter says that he has to buy an occasional new cigar. But he gets it on sale.

*Schloss on another occasion said of Buffett:* "There's never been anything like him . . . the continued growth will be very hard. Maybe he'll merge it [Berkshire] with Canada."[74]

## EARNINGS, EARNINGS, EARNINGS

Earnings, or a promise of future earnings, give stocks their value:

*"We like stocks that generate high returns on invested capital where there is a strong likelihood that it will continue to do so. For example, the last time we bought Coca-Cola, it was selling at about 23 times earnings. Using our purchase price and today's earnings, that makes it about 5 times earnings. It's really the interaction*

*of capital employed, the return on that capital, and future capital generated versus the purchase price today.*"[75]

~

*"If the business does well, the stock eventually follows."*[76]

Buffett explains that buying the stock of companies with strong earnings is a hedge against inflation:

*"An irony of inflation-induced financial requirements is that the highly profitable companies—generally the best credits—require relatively little debt capital. But the laggards in profitability never can get enough. Lenders understand this problem much better than they did a decade ago—and are correspondingly less willing to let capital-hungry, low-profitability enterprises leverage themselves to the sky."*[77]

One fiscal quarter does not an earnings trend make, as Buffett noted while discussing the direction of Salomon Inc.'s business:

*"As long as we can make an annual 15 percent return on equity, I don't worry about one quarter's results."*[78]

## LOOK FORWARD, NOT BACK

*"Pension fund managers continue to make investment decisions with their eyes firmly fixed on the rearview mirror. This general fight-the-last-war approach has*

*proven costly in the past and will likely prove equally costly this time around."*[79]

~

*"Of course, the investor of today does not profit from yesterday's growth."*[80]

## AVOID RISK

Author Timothy Vick explains that "what Warren is always trying to do is minimize his losses to absolute zero. People say Buffett is a great stock picker. I see him as a great avoider [of poor investments]."[81]

*"I put heavy weight on certainty. . . . If you do that, the whole idea of a risk factor doesn't make any sense to me. You don't do it where you take a significant risk. But it's not risky to buy securities at a fraction of what they're worth."*[82]

Buffett often uses the *Washington Post* as an example of a risk-free investment. In 1973, the market price for the *Post* was $80 million, and the company had no debt:

*"If you asked anyone in the business what [the* Post's*] properties were worth, they'd have said $400 million or something like that. You could have an auction in the middle of the Atlantic Ocean at 2:00 in the morning, and you would have had people show up and bid that much for them. And it was being run by honest and able people*

*who all had a significant part of their net worth in the business. It was ungodly safe. It wouldn't have bothered me to put my whole net worth in it. Not in the least."*[83]

~

*"Risk comes from not knowing what you are doing."*[84]

This said, the insurance industry is all about taking risk and occasionally taking a "mega-cat" (short for "mega-catastrophe") hit. This is especially true in the reinsurance business. Buffett's insurance group has provided insurance for the 2002 Winter Olympics, the life of boxer Mike Tyson, and lots of lotteries. Berkshire continues to write major terrorism reinsurance policies following September 11, 2001.

*"When a major quake occurs in an urban area or a winter storm rages across Europe, light a candle for us."*[85]

The Berkshire Hathaway Reinsurance group lost $2.2 billion as a result of the 9/11 terrorist attacks on the World Trade Center. It took another blow in 2005 when underwriting went into the red due to $2.5 billion in losses from hurricanes Katrina, Rita, and Wilma. The trick to survival is to have a strong enough company to withstand occasional large-magnitude setbacks. Even though 2006 was a quiet year, hurricanes and weather events are becoming ever more problematic for insurance companies:

*"Were the terrible hurricane seasons of 2004–05 aberrations? Or were they our planet's first warning that the climate of the twenty-first century will differ materially from what we've seen in the past? If the answer to the second question is yes, 2006 will soon be perceived as a misleading period of calm preceding a serious of devastating storms. These could rock the insurance industry. It's naïve to think of Katrina as anything close to a worst-case event."*[86]

There is a big difference between calculated risk and wild-eyed hope:

*"Long ago, Sir Isaac Newton gave us three laws of motion, which were the work of genius. But Isaac's talents didn't extend to investing. He lost a bundle in the South Sea Bubble, explaining later, 'I can calculate the movement of the stars, but not the madness of men.' If he had not been traumatized by the loss, Sir Isaac might well have gone on to discover the Fourth Law of Motion:* For investors as a whole, returns decrease as motion increases."[87]

## DON'T GAMBLE

*"The propensity to gamble is always increased by a large prize versus a small entry fee, no matter how poor the true odds may be. That's why Las Vegas casinos advertise big jackpots and why state lotteries headline big prizes."*[88]

Some of futures markets' products are nothing more than gambling games with a big skim for the casino owners:

> *"And the more the activity, the greater the cost to the public and the greater the amount of money that will be left behind by them to be spread among the brokerage industry."*[89]

If you are drawn to the casino, watch what you drink:

> *"You're dealing with a lot of silly people in the marketplace; it's like a great big casino, and everyone else is boozing. If you can stick with Pepsi [or Coca-Cola], you should be okay."*[90]

Marshall Weinberg of the brokerage firm of Gruntal & Co. told about going to lunch with Buffett in Manhattan: "He had an exceptional ham-and-cheese sandwich. A few days later, we were going out again. He said, 'Let's go back to that restaurant.' I said, 'But we were just there.' He said, 'Precisely. Why take a risk with another place? We know exactly what we're going to get.' That," said Weinberg, "is what Warren looks for in stocks, too. He only invests in companies where the odds are great that they will not disappoint."[91]

> *"People would rather be promised a [presumably] winning lottery ticket next week than an opportunity to get rich slowly."*[92]

Gambling in the market is treacherous for investors, and it has a negative effect on the national economy:

> *"We do not need more people gambling on the non-essential instruments identified with the stock market in the country, nor brokers who encourage them to do so. What we need are investors and advisers who look at the long-term prospects for an enterprise and invest accordingly. We need the intelligent commitment of investment capital, not leveraged market wagers. The propensity to operate in the intelligent, prosocial sectors of capital markets is deterred, not enhanced, by an active and exciting casino operating in somewhat the same arena, utilizing somewhat similar language, and serviced by the same workforce."*[93]

## WATCH FOR UNUSUAL CIRCUMSTANCES

> *"Great investment opportunities come around when excellent companies are surrounded by unusual circumstances that cause the stock to be misappraised."*[94]

## DON'T BE SURPRISED BY CIRCUMSTANCES

> *"It's only when the tide goes out that you learn who's been swimming naked."*[95]

## AVOID EXCESSIVE DEBT

Buffett calls borrowed money a dagger tied to a company's steering wheel pointed straight at its heart:

*"You will someday hit a pothole."* [96]

Charlie Munger also has an opinion on debt: "Warren and I are chicken about buying stocks on margin. There's always a slight chance of catastrophe when you own securities pledged to others. The ideal is to borrow in a way no temporary thing can disturb you." [97]

Buffett also says the ever-increasing U.S. trade deficit is a dangerously accruing debt that is secured by U.S. assets:

*"Our riches are our curse in our attempts to attain a trade balance. If we were less well-off, commercial realities would constrain our trade deficit. Because we are rich, however, we can continue to trade earning properties for consumable trinkets. We are much like a wealthy farm family that annually sells acreage so that it can sustain a lifestyle unwarranted by its current output. Until the plantation is gone, it's all pleasure and no pain. In the end, however, the family will have traded the life of an owner for the life of a tenant farmer."* [98]

Buffett has suggested a solution to the trade problem: a system of issuing import certificates when a certain value of goods is exported, whereby it would be necessary to have a certificate to import that same value of goods into the United States. The exporter could sell or trade his or her certificates to an importer. A buy-sell-or-barter system for the certificates would evolve, and imports and exports would always be of equal value. Buffett put forth his scheme in an op-ed piece in the *Washington Post* in 1987. Perhaps because the proposal would increase import prices and reduce U.S. consumption of foreign goods (getting a grip on our national impulse to consume more than we produce), there was no stampede to adopt Buffett's plan.

## LOOK FOR SCREAMING BARGAINS

Authors who have written about Buffett's investment style tell how he measures the stream of cash that the company generates today and into the future, then, using a reasonable interest rate, discounts the cash flow back to the present. Is it possible that Buffett just clicks the calculations off in his head? Maybe. There seems to be no paper trail:

"Warren talks about these discounted cash flows . . . I've never seen him do one," Munger huffed.

"It's true," replied Buffett. "If [the value of a company] doesn't just scream out at you, it's too close."[99]

## ARBITRAGE WHEN POSSIBLE

When Buffett's approach to investing is distilled to its simplest form, his activities fall into three major categories:

1. *General Investments.*  Undervalued, good-quality securities that provide a comfortable margin of safety.
2. *Controlling Investment.*  Companies in which Berkshire has controlling interest or full ownership. In some cases, such as with the original Berkshire Hathaway and with GEICO, Buffett moved progressively from a general investment to full ownership.
3. *Arbitrages or Special Situations.*  Opportunities that can occur during mergers, acquisitions, reorganizations, liquidations, misalignments in currency or commodity markets, and so forth.

"Because my mother isn't here tonight, I'll even confess to you that I have been an arbitrageur," Buffett said at a business seminar.[100] Buffett learned arbitrage during his early days at Graham-Newman. In its pure forv m, arbitrage is buying at a low price in one market and selling at a higher price in another. Buffett uses arbitrage when one company announces the acquisition of another company at a price higher than the current market quote:

> *"We look at the arbitrage deal, once something is announced. We look at what they've announced, what we think it will be worth, what we will have to pay, how long we're going to be in. We try to calculate the*

*probability it will go through. That is the calculation: the name [of the companies involved] doesn't make much difference."*[101]

Early in 1998 Buffett announced that Berkshire had collected 129.7 million ounces of silver, which represented 30 percent of the world's above-ground inventory. Buffett started buying around July 25, 1997, a day when silver futures contracts were at $4.32 per ounce, the lowest price they had been in 650 years. Berkshire's silver cost him $650 million. By February 1998, when he announced the silver purchase, his investment had grown to $850 million.

This is the largest single silver position since the Hunt brothers apparently tried to corner the silver market in 1980. Despite the astounding size of Buffett's stash, it only represents about 2 percent of Berkshire's capital.

Buffett first became interest in silver back in the 1960s when the metal was about to be demonetized by the U.S. government. Although he didn't own the metal after that, he kept an eye on silver's fundamentals. When bullion inventories fell dramatically because of an excess of user demand over mine production and reclamation, Buffett and Munger decided that equilibrium would recur at some point and the price would be higher.

Equilibrium did arrive, but it took a good long time to happen. At the 2000 annual meeting, Munger explained,

"It's been a dull ride." However, silver prices slowly rebounded, reaching $8.83 an ounce in 2005 and $13.73 an ounce by February 2007. In nine years, Buffett's silver had tripled in value to nearly $1.3 billion.

## BE PATIENT

*"In investments, there's no such thing as a called strike. You can stand there at the plate and the pitcher can throw a ball right down the middle; and if it's General Motors at 47 and you don't know enough to decide on General Motors at 47, you let it go right on by and no one's going to call a strike. The only way you can have a strike is to swing and miss."*[102]

Buffett said on another occasion:

*"I've never swung at a ball while it's still in the pitcher's glove."*[103]

~

*"You do things when the opportunities come along. I've had periods in my life when I've had a bundle of ideas come along, and I've had long dry spells. If I get an idea next week, I'll do something. If not, I won't do a damn thing."*[104]

~

*"You could be somewhere where the mail was delayed three weeks and do just fine investing."*[105]

# THINK FOR YOURSELF

Munger says that coming from Omaha, Buffett absorbed the attitude of a self-reliant pioneer: "Buffett believes successful investment is intrinsically independent in nature." [106]

~

How much attention does Buffett pay to the recommendation of brokers?

*"Never ask the barber if you need a haircut."* [107]

As for stock market forecasters:

*"Forecasts usually tell us more of the forecaster than of the future."* [108]

A constant stream of people ask Buffett to invest in their ideas. To most, he says:

*"With my idea and your money, we'll do okay."* [109]

Buffett and Munger make a committee of two; and at times, even Charlie seems extraneous:

*"My idea of a group decision is to look in the mirror."* [110]

~

*"If [former] Fed Chairman Alan Greenspan were to whisper to me what his monetary policy was going to be over the next two years, it wouldn't change one thing I do."* [111]

Especially don't listen to a computer:

*"The more instruments that are designed, the smarter the players have to be."*[112]

~

*"You have to think for yourself. It always amazes me how high-IQ people mindlessly imitate. I never get good ideas talking to other people."*[113]

## HAVE THE RIGHT TOOLS

Buffett's suggestion to the independent investor is:

*"You should have a knowledge of how business operates and the language of business [accounting], some enthusiasm for the subject, and qualities of temperament, which may be more important than IQ points. These will enable you to think independently and to avoid various forms of mass hysteria that infect the investment markets from time to time."*[114]

Understanding the fundamentals of accounting is a form of self-defense:

*"When managers want to get across the facts of the business to you, it can be done within the rules of accounting. Unfortunately, when they want to play games, at least in some industries, it can also be done within the rules of accounting. If you can't recognize the differences, you shouldn't be in the equity-picking business."*[115]

# BE WARY OF WALL STREET

*"Wall Street is the only place that people ride to in a Rolls Royce to get advice from those who take the subway."*[116]

~

*"Full-time professionals in other fields, let's say dentists, bring a lot to the layman. But in aggregate, people get nothing for their money from professional money managers."*[117]

~

*"Wall Street likes to characterize the proliferation of frenzied financial games as a sophisticated, prosocial activity facilitating the fine-tuning of a complex economy. But the truth is otherwise: Short-term transactions frequently act as an invisible foot, kicking society in the shins."*[118]

Options traders are a favorite Buffett target:

*"It has always been a fantasy of mine that a boatload of 25 brokers would be shipwrecked and struggle to an island from which there could be no rescue. Faced with developing an economy that would maximize their consumption and pleasure, would they, I wonder, assign 20 of their number to produce food, clothing, shelter, etc., while setting 5 to trading options endlessly on the future output of the 20?"*[119]

~

*"To many on Wall Street, both companies and stocks are seen only as raw materials for trades."*[120]

Charlie Munger says he agrees with John Maynard Keynes, who called investment management a "low calling."

*"Warren and I are a little different, in that we actually run businesses and allocate capital to them. Keynes atoned for his 'sins' by making money for his college and serving his nation. I do my outside activities to atone, and Warren uses his investment success to be a great teacher. And we love to make money for the people who trusted us early on, when we were young and poor."*[121]

## ONLY BUY SECURITIES THAT YOU UNDERSTAND

*"Investment must be rational; if you can't understand it, don't do it."*[122]

~

Asked about the use of derivatives as an investment vehicle, Buffett said that the danger is twofold: Derivatives are seldom well understood by investors, and they tend to involve heavy leverage:

*"When you combine ignorance and borrowed money, the consequences can get interesting."*[123]

~

*"I want to be able to explain my mistakes. This means I do only the things I completely understand."*[124]

Buffett had a couple of highly profitable years investing in direct currencies. These came from forward contracts, which are derivatives:

> *"Why, you may wonder, are we fooling around with such potentially toxic material? The answer is that derivatives, just like stocks and bonds, are sometimes wildly mispriced."*[125]

Buffett says that over the years he has on rare occasion delved into derivatives, usually for large dollar amounts. He personally manages the tricky investments, and so far they have produced pretax profits in the hundreds of millions of dollars.

Berkshire owned four million shares of General Foods Corporation and, in October 1985, captured profits of $332 million when the company was sold to Philip Morris Co. General Foods owns familiar brand names like Tang, Jell-O, and Kool-Aid. Buffett said:

> *"I can understand Kool-Aid."*

## AN OLD DOG PROWLS NEW MARKETS

What goes for individual stocks also goes for stock markets. However, this is an area in which Buffett has changed. He once said:

> *"It's hard enough to understand the peculiarities and complexities of the culture in which you've been raised,*

*much less a variety of others. Anyway, most of our shareholders have to pay their bills in U.S. dollars."*[126]

Additionally, the U.S. equity market is huge:

*"If I can't make money in a $5 trillion market, it may be a little bit of wishful thinking to think that all I have to do is get a few thousand miles away and I'll start showing my stuff."*[127]

Gradually, Buffett softened his attitude toward foreign investments. Partly, this was because of a scarcity of alluring investments in the United States; but it also is related to his views on U.S. trade imbalance and the negative impact that eventually will have on the strength of the dollar.

In 2002, Buffett entered $11 billion worth of forward contracts to deliver U.S. dollars against other currencies; the contracts were profitable to the tune of $2.2 billion. However, because of accounting rules related to long-term currency contracts, earnings were distorted in every quarter. Buffett began reducing his currency positions somewhat and partially offset this by purchasing equities whose prices are denominated in various foreign currencies and that earn a substantial portion of their profits in other countries. By 2006, he was out of the direct foreign exchange market because the profitable differentials were gone.

On a 2002 trip to Britain, he told the *Sunday Telegraph* that he was looking for a "big deal" in that country.

> *"We are hunting elephant. . . . We have got an elephant gun and it's loaded"*[128]

Some of his forays in Great Britain include the liquor company Allied Domecq PLC, Yorkshire Electricity, and the grocery chain Tesco. He also bought 4 percent of the Korean steel company Posco and snapped up several Israeli technology companies.

At the 2006 annual meeting, Buffett said that if he were starting over again, he would invest worldwide.

## PETROCHINA

PetroChina is the world's fourth-largest oil company measured by market capitalization, ranking just below Royal Dutch Shell. Berkshire holds 2.3 billion shares, which amounts to 1.3 percent of the foreign ownership of the company. Buffett paid $488 million for the shares, which in late 2006 had grown in value to $3.3 billion.

PetroChina's dominant shareholder is the government of China. This fact, plus a wave of indignation over human rights atrocities occurring in the West African nation of Sudan, prompted Buffett to post a commentary of Berkshire's web site. Activists claim that PetroChina has major oil investments in Sudan, which provides revenues that sustain an abusive, authoritarian government. There have been calls for Buffett to divest his PetroChina shares.

In the web site commentary, Buffett noted that he's seen no evidence that PetroChina has operations in Sudan, even though the nation of China does.

> *"The Chinese government's activities can be attributed to neither PetroChina nor the other major Chinese companies the government controls, such as China Mobile, China Life, and China Telecom. Subsidiaries have no ability to control the policies of their parent."*[129]

Buffett goes on to caution protestors to be careful of unintended consequences. If China sold off its Sudan investments, it would be forced to do so at a very low price; and the most likely buyer would be the Sudanese government.

> *"After such a transaction the Sudanese government would be* better *off financially, with its oil revenues substantially increased. Since oil is a fungible product, Sudanese output would be sold in world markets just as oil from Iraq was sold under Saddam Hussein and just as oil is now sold by Iran. Proponents of the Chinese government's divesting should ask the*

most important question in economics, 'And then what?'"[130]

# AN EXPANDING CIRCLE OF COMPETENCE

This is how you expand a circle of competence:

*"Draw a circle around the businesses you understand and then eliminate those that fail to qualify on the basis of value, good management, and limited exposure to hard times."*[131]

Next:

*"I would take one industry at a time and develop some expertise in half a dozen. I would not take the conventional wisdom now about any industries as meaning a damn thing. I would try to think it through.*

*"If I were looking at an insurance company or a paper company, I would put myself in the frame of mind that I had just inherited that company and it was the only asset my family was ever going to own.*

*"What would I do with it? What am I thinking about? What am I worried about? Who are my competitors? Who are my customers? Go out and talk to them. Find out the strengths and weaknesses of this particular company versus other ones.*

*"If you've done that, you may understand the business better than the management."*[132]

~

*"Anybody who tells you they can value, you know, all the stocks in Value Live and on the board must have a very inflated idea of their own ability because it's not that easy. But if you spend your time focusing on some industries, you'll learn a lot about valuation."*[133]

Staying within his circle of competence means that Buffett will miss certain good investments simply because he didn't have the skill or knowledge to evaluate the companies involved:

*"I missed the play in cellular because cellular is outside of my circle of competence."*[134]

A circle of competence can serve over a lifetime. In 1995, Berkshire acquired the 49 percent of GEICO it didn't already own. Buffett became interested in GEICO when he discovered that his professor, Ben Graham, was its chairman:

*"When I was 20, I invested well over half of my net worth in GEICO."*[135]

When asked why he invested in insurance, a notoriously roller-coaster business:

*"Sometimes it's a good business—and that's not very often—and sometimes it's a terrible business."*[136]

It depends on how the risk is managed:

*"I can go into an emergency ward and write life insurance if you let me charge enough of a premium."*[137]

NOTE: Buffett is known for his skill at investing insurance float, the money that has been collected in premiums but not yet paid out in claims.

Buffett used to say:

*"Our principles are valid when applied to technology stocks, but we don't know how to do it. If we are going to lose your money, we want to be able to get up here next year and explain how we did it. I'm sure Bill Gates would apply the same principles. He understands technology the way I understand Coca-Cola or Gillette. I'm sure he looks for a margin of safety. I'm sure he would approach it like he was owning a business and not just a stock. So our principles can work for any technology. We just aren't the ones to do it. If we can't find things within our circle of competence, we won't expand the circle. We'll wait."*[138]

Charlie Munger has his own ideas on this subject: "About circle of competence—have three baskets—In, Out, and Too Tough. Toss a lot into the Too Tough basket."[139]

Perhaps it was his growing friendship and discussions with Bill Gates that prompted Buffett to drift into a higher level of technology. (Gates joined the Berkshire board of directors in 2005.) In 1999, Buffett acquired a

6.8 percent stake in Great Lakes Chemical Corp. and an 8.1 percent position in TCA Cable TV. In 2002, Buffett made a $500 million investment in Level 3 Communications, which operates a national high-speed network that transmits voice and data communications. One reason Buffett felt confident about Level 3 is because it was founded by a subsidiary of Omaha-based Peter Kiewit Sons Inc., and Buffett's friend Walter Scott Jr. (and Berkshire board member) serves as chairman:

> *"Sometimes you're outside your core competency. Level 3 is one of those times; but I've made a bet on the people, and I feel I understand the people. There was a time when people made a bet on me."*[140]

Buffett kept on expanding his circle, buying Nextel debt and preferred shares and purchasing TTI, the privately owned leading distributor of passive, interconnect, and electromagnetic components. Based in Fort Worth, Texas, TTI is the seventh-largest component distributor in the world.

## BUY READING GLASSES

How does Buffett determine the value of a business? He reads a lot.

> *"I read annual reports of the company I'm looking at, and I read the annual reports of the competitors—that is the main source of material."*[141]

When he first took an interest in GEICO, this is what Buffett did:

> *"I read a lot. I was over at the library. . . . I started with Bests' [insurance rating service], looking at a lot of companies, reading some books about it, reading annual reports, talking to [insurance specialists], talking to managements when I could."*[142]

Munger concurs that reading is essential: "In my whole life, I have known no wise people—none, zero—[who don't read]. You would be amazed at how much Warren reads. . . . My children probably think of me as a book with two legs sticking out."[143]

Don't blame yourself, Buffett says, if you don't understand everything:

> *"It's not impossible to write [an accounting] footnote explaining deferred acquisition costs in life insurance or whatever you want to do. You can write it so you can understand it. If it's written so you can't understand it, I'm very suspicious. I won't invest in a company if I can't understand the footnote because I know they don't want me to understand it."*[144]

## BECOME AN INVESTIGATIVE REPORTER

*Washington Post* reporter Bob Woodward (of Watergate fame) once asked Buffett how he analyzed stocks:

> *"Investing is reporting. I told him to imagine he had been assigned an in-depth article about his own paper. He'd ask a lot of questions and dig up a lot of facts. He'd know the* Washington Post. *And that's all there is to it."*[145]

Buffett's research takes curious turns. He once sat behind the cash register at Ross's, a favorite Omaha steakhouse, counting how many customers used American Express cards.[146] Sometimes the research doesn't even seem like research:

> *"I remember I went to see* Mary Poppins *at a theater on Broadway at 45th [Street] at about 2:00 in the afternoon. I had a little attache case and everything. I got up to this woman at the ticket booth and said, 'I've got a kid around here someplace.' I was going to see if this [movie] could be run over and over again in the future."*[147]

## KEEP IT SIMPLE

When a friend suggested Buffett try his hand at real estate, he replied:

> *"Why should I buy real estate when the stock market is so easy?"*[148]

~

> *"[Value investing] ideas seem so simple and common-place. It seems like a waste to go to school and get a Ph.D. in economics. It's a little like spending eight*

*years in divinity school and having someone tell you the Ten Commandments are all that matter.*"[149]

When asked how he and Munger perform "due diligence" on companies they buy, Buffett said:

*"If you have to go through too much investigation, something is wrong."*[150]

Charlie said they were once subpoenaed for their staff papers on an acquisition: "There weren't any papers. There wasn't any staff," Munger said.[151]

In 1986, Berkshire Hathaway ran a newspaper advertisement seeking companies to buy. It read:

*"We use no staff, and we don't need to discuss your company with consultants, investment bankers, commercial bankers, etc. You will deal only with Charles Munger, vice chairman of Berkshire, and with me."*[152]

～

*"All there is to investing is picking good stocks at good times and staying with them as long as they remain good companies."*[153]

～

*"Talking at business schools, I always say [students] would be better off if, when they got out of school, they got a ticket with 20 punches on it. And every time they make an investment decision, it uses up a punch.*

*You'll never use up all 20 punches if you save them for the great ideas."*[154]

NOTE: *Forbes* columnist Mark Hulbert ran some numbers and determined that if you remove Buffett's 15 best decisions from the hundreds of others, his long-term performance would be mediocre.[155]

Charlie Munger says this about the simplicity theory: "If you believe what Warren says, you could teach the whole [portfolio management] course in a couple of weeks."[156]

~

# THINK BIG

At the beginning of a Berkshire Hathaway annual meeting several years ago, Buffett tapped the microphone to see if it was on:

*"Testing . . . one million . . . two million . . . three million."*[157]

~

*"I made a study back when I ran an investment partnership of all our larger investments versus the smaller investments. The larger investments always did better than the smaller investments. There is a threshold of examination and criticism and knowledge that has to be overcome or reached in making a big decision that you can get sloppy about on small decisions. Somebody*

*says, 'I bought a hundred shares of this or that because I heard about it at a party the other night.' Well, there is that tendency with small decisions to think you can do it for not very good reasons."*[158]

~

*"I can't be involved in 50 or 75 things. That's a Noah's Ark way of investing—you end up with a zoo that way. I like to put meaningful amounts of money in a few things."*[159]

Although Buffett says small companies can offer exceptional growth, such companies are inappropriate for a holding company of Berkshire's size:

*"We're looking for 747s, not model airplanes."*[160]

~

*"I'm like a basketball coach. I go out on the street and look for seven-footers. If some guy comes up to me and says, 'I'm five-six, but you ought to see me handle the ball,' I'm not interested."*[161]

Large or small, the company must perform:

*"I'd rather have a $10 million business making 15 percent than a $100 million business making 5 percent."*[162]

# KNOW WHAT YOU'RE LOOKING FOR

The Berkshire Hathaway advertisement for possible acquisitions that ran in the *Wall Street Journal* constituted a virtual checklist for value investors.

"Here's what we are looking for," the ad read:[163]

1. Large purchases (at least $10 million of after-tax earnings, and preferably much more).

   NOTE: Individual investors can ignore the first one. It is there because small purchases can't make a blip on Berkshire's bottom line. The fact that individual investors can profit from smaller investments is an advantage, since it gives a much wider range of stocks from which to choose.

2. Demonstrated consistent earning power (future projections are of little interest to us, nor are "turnaround" situations).

3. Businesses earning good returns on equity while employing little or no debt.

4. Management in place (we can't supply it).

   NOTE: A subtle way of saying *good* management in place.

5. Simple businesses (if there's a lot of technology, we won't understand it).

6. An offering price (we don't want to waste our time or that of the seller by talking, even preliminarily, about a transaction when price is unknown).

NOTE: Luckily for small investors, Mr. Market shows up every workday with an offering price.

Each year in Berkshire Hathaway's annual report, Buffett publishes a similar list of traits of a business that would interest him. Occasionally the list is cast aside. It is, he says:

> *"a lot like selecting a wife. You can thoughtfully establish certain qualities you'd like her to have, then all of a sudden, you meet someone and you do it."*[164]

## DON'T SWEAT THE MATH

Buffett says that because he never studied calculus, he's forced to agree with those who say that higher math skill is not needed for successful investing:

> *"If calculus were required, I'd have to go back to delivering papers. I've never seen any need for algebra. Essentially, you're trying to figure out the value of a business. It's true that you have to divide by the number of shares outstanding, so division is required. If you were going out to buy a farm or an apartment house or a dry cleaning establishment, I really don't think you'd have to take someone along to do calculus. Whether you made the right purchase or not would depend on the future earning ability of that enterprise, and then relating that to the price you are being asked for the asset."*[165]

~

*"Read Ben Graham and Phil Fisher, read annual reports, but don't do equations with Greek letters in them."*[166]

If higher math is unimportant in selecting stocks, why are academic and professional journals dense with quantitative analysis? Buffett replied:

*"Every priesthood does it. How could you be on top if no one is on the bottom?"*[167]

Buffett's mathless philosophy did not come naturally. He developed it after he'd tried everything else:

*"I used to chart all kinds of stocks, the more numbers the better."*[168]

As a teenager, Buffett was fascinated by technical information. This interest led to the publication of Buffett's first article. He was 17:

*"There was an item [in* Barron's*] saying that if we would send along a description of how we used their statistical material, they would publish some of them and pay $5. I wrote up something about how I used odd-lot figures. That $5 was the only money I ever made using statistics."*[169]

# ADMIRE FRUGALITY

> *"Whenever I read about some company undertaking a cost-cutting program, I know it's not a company that really knows what costs are all about. Spurts don't work in this area. The really good manager does not wake up in the morning and say, 'This is the day I'm going to cut costs,' any more than he wakes up and decides to practice breathing."*[170]

~

Berkshire Hathaway owned about 7 percent of the stock of San Francisco–based Wells Fargo. News reached Munger that Wells Fargo CEO Carl Reichardt discovered that one of his executives wanted to buy a Christmas tree for the office. Reichardt told him to buy it with his own money.

"When we heard that," said Munger, "we bought more stock."[171]

Berkshire now owns 13.66% of wells Fargo.

For Buffett, frugality begins at home. At the 1996 Berkshire annual meeting, he observed:

> *"Your board has collectively lost 100 pounds in the last year. They must have been trying to live on their director's fees."*[172]

~

Buffett wrote the foreword to Alan C. (Ace) Greenberg's book, *Memos from the Chairman* (Workman, 1996), in which a fictional character, Haimchinkel Malintz Anaynikal, urged Bear Stearns employees not to waste resources. Wrote Buffett:

*"Haimchinkel is my kind of guy—cheap, smart, opinionated. I just wish I'd met him earlier in life, when, in the foolishness of my youth, I used to discard paper clips. But it's never too late, and I now slavishly follow and preach his principles."*[173]

The quest for quality and the need for frugality need not cancel each other out, as Buffett noted when talking about programming at ABC:

*"The funny thing is, better shows don't cost that much more than lousy shows."*[174]

Sports shows also could be aired for less money:

*"My guess is that the quality of football would be identical if we'd been paying 20 percent less for the football rights. It's just that all the football players would be earning a little less money. Ty Cobb played for $20,000 a year. In the end, if there's 20 percent less money available for sports programming, it will largely come out of the players."*[175]

Buffett also applies thriftiness to his own financial affairs. He and former Capital Cities/ABC chairman Thomas Murphy had walk-on parts on the ABC television soap opera *All My Children* with soap queen Susan Lucci in

1993. Buffett and Murphy were each paid about $300 for their performances.

When handed his check, Murphy said, "I'm going to frame this." Buffett said, "I'm going to frame the stub."[176]

## SET REALISTIC GOALS

Buffett says a growth rate of 15 percent per year is realistic, though not always easy for him to achieve:

> *"If we are to have a 15 percent gain, we have to make $400 million [a year] before tax, or $300 million net, which is about a million a day—and I'm spending today here."*[177]

NOTE: In fact, he usually does achieve it. Berkshire's book value has grown at an annual average rate of 21.5 percent between 1963 and 2005. However, size is a drag. Buffett only achieved more than a 15 percent gain in one year since 2000.

## FACE FACTS

Don't take the performance of your stock personally. After all:

> *"A stock doesn't know you own it."*[178]

Buffett has good reason for his interest in entertainment and leisure-oriented businesses:

> *"The market will pay you better to entertain than to educate."*[179]

CASE IN POINT: Berkshire's *World Book* encyclopedia has difficulty delivering the same stellar returns that Buffett's investment in the Disney Company achieved.

Gold, Buffett says, is nonproductive:

*"It gets dug out of the ground in Africa or someplace. We melt it down, dig another hole, bury it again, and pay people to stand around guarding it. It has no utility. Anyone watching from Mars would be scratching their head."* [180]

When Buffett is asked at Berkshire annual meetings why he doesn't split the company's high-priced shares, people murmur to one another, "Here comes the pizza story."

The question, Buffett says, reminds him of a diner who asks the pizza maker to cut his pie into four slices rather than eight, since he "couldn't possibly eat eight." [181]

## HE TELLS THEM BUT THEY DON'T LISTEN

Every year in Berkshire Hathaway's annual report and again at the shareholder's meeting, Buffett warns investors not to expect Berkshire's performance to continue at former speeds:

1985: "I can guarantee we will not do as well as in the past," Buffett told shareholders at the annual meeting.

"I still think we may be able to do better than American industry as a whole."[182]

In 1984, Berkshire's gain was a weak 13.6 percent, compared to a 22 percent average annual increase in the previous 20 years. In 1986, Berkshire chalked up a 48.2 percent gain.

1992: Charlie Munger told *Business Week:* "Size at a certain point gets to be an anchor, which drags you down. We always knew that it would."[183] Berkshire's share price rose 20.3 percent in 1992.

1995: At Berkshire Hathaway's annual meeting, Buffett again cautioned: "The future performance of Berkshire Hathaway won't come close to matching the performance of the past." He explained that "a fat wallet, however, is the enemy of superior results." And anyhow, "We don't have to keep getting rich at the same rate."[184]

1999 to 2005: During this period, Buffett's prediction began to come true—the per-share book value only increased 6.96 percent, compared to 21.5 percent from 1964 to 2005, the time Buffett has controlled the company. Yet Buffett did best the S&P 500, which from 1999 to 2005 grew its book value by only 3.2 percent. The S&P 500 numbers are pretax, while Buffett's are after-tax, which means he actually did considerably better.

2007: In 1996, Berkshire's A shares traded as high as $38,000. By mid-1996, the shares had retreated to $32,000. By spring of 2007, a single A share traded for $108,000.

# EXPECT CHANGE

*"Anything that can't go on forever will end."*[185]

~

When asked what he thought of the wave of U.S. corporate downsizing, Buffett noted that U.S. industry has always tried to do more with less. Change is unavoidable, but:

> *"It's no fun being a horse when the tractor comes along, or the blacksmith when the car comes along."*[186]

Turn the question backward, says Charlie Munger: "Name a business that has been ruined by downsizing. I can't name one. Name a company that has been ruined by bloat. I can name dozens."[187]

Buffett agrees that it is sometimes wise to look at problems from the opposite direction:

> *"It's like singing country western songs backward. That way you get your home back, your auto back, your wife back, and so forth."*[188]

Nevertheless, Buffett and Munger like industries in which change is limited, or at least manageable. Said Buffett:

> *"Take chewing gum, for example. Folks chew the same way today that they did 20 years ago. Nobody's come up with a new technique for that."*[189]

# BE CAPABLE OF CHANGE

When asked why he abandoned some value investing principles, Buffett replied:

> *"As we work with larger sums of money, it simply is not possible to stay with those subworking capital types of situations. It requires learning more about what's going to produce steady and increasing flows of cash in the future—if you are working with small sums of money, you don't even have to work that hard. We [at Graham-Newman] used to have a one-page sheet where you put down all the numbers on a company; and if it met certain tests of book value, working capital, and earnings, you bought it. It was that simple."*[190]

Buffett did not abruptly abandon certain teachings of Graham and his co-author David Dodd:

> *"I evolved. I didn't go from ape to human or human to ape in a nice even manner."*[191]

## BABY BERKSHIRE SHARES

During the 1990s, Berkshire Hathaway's share price rode on the wings of a soaring market, finally peaking at just over $38,000 in March 1996 (shares traded for $8,550 in mid-1989). Despite the dizzying climb, Warren Buffett stood firm on his refusal to split shares, a step that would make it easier for new investors to buy and existing investors to sell. He said he didn't want Berkshire in the hands of speculators, and the most effective deterrent he could think of was a steep share price. Buffett signed birthday cards with the line, "May you live until Berkshire shares split."

Buffett held true to his word; but within a few weeks of the 1996 price peak, outside events compelled him to create the moral equivalent of a split. That spring, Buffett announced he would issue B shares, or secondary common shares, of Berkshire Hathaway stock. The new shares were issued at one-thirtieth the price of the existing, or A, shares. The only features that make B shares secondary were the lack of voting rights and the fact that B shareholders are ineligible for the charitable giving program Berkshire used at the time. Voting rights are unimportant since Buffett and Munger have enough shares to outvote all other holders. And who in his or her right mind would vote against Buffett and Munger anyway?

The advantage to A shareholders is that they can convert to 30 B shares at any time, no matter what the prices of the two shares are. B shareholders, however, are not allowed to convert to A shares, even if holders own 30 of them.

As Buffett anticipated, arbitrage action between the two types of shares has almost always kept A and B prices in a 1-to-30 balance. If B shares ever rise above one/thirtieth the price of an A, someone—perhaps a New York Stock Exchange specialist or Buffett himself—buys A shares and coverts them into B. This pushes the price of the B shares down. If the B shares sell for less than one/thirtieth an A share, investors buy Bs instead of As, and demand drives the price of B shares higher.

What made Buffett modify his plans was a scheme by several investment firms to create unit trusts from a pool composed entirely of Berkshire shares. Investors would buy the bite-size portions of Berkshire for $1,000 per unit and pay annual fees, plus up-front commissions of as much as 5 percent. Investors could hold the units until a 10-year maturity date or trade them on the New York Stock Exchange like any other security. The unit trusts were to be marketed to small investors hoping to participate in the remarkable gains enjoyed by those who had discovered Berkshire Hathaway early on.

Speculation is speculation, even if it is once removed, in Buffett's view; "We do not want people to come in and think it's a hot stock and it will be a lot higher in a year."[192]

Or, more specifically: "There are people who think it (Berkshire's phenomenal share price growth) can happen again from this kind of base, and it's mathematically impossible," Buffett said. "We don't want to appeal subliminally to people who harbor these hopes."[193]

Critics said Buffett's controlling nature caused his reaction. Others said he was just being consistent. Buffett always said he wanted dedicated shareholders. "It gets down to attracting the highest-grade shareholder we can get."[194]

In a letter of protest to Five Sigma Investment Partners of Bala Cynwyd, Pennsylvania, one of the firms that proposed such a unit trust, Charlie Munger wrote: "Your trust . . . would entice many small investors into an investment unsuitable for them and overwhelmingly likely to leave large numbers feeling disappointed and abused."

Munger added: "Berkshire's stock price is now risky because [of] dramatic appreciation . . . since 1992 at a rate far higher than any increase in the stock's intrinsic value. . . . If he were asked by a friend or family member whether he advised a new purchase of Berkshire shares at the current price, Mr. Buffett would answer, 'No.'"[195] Munger said he feared aggressive sales efforts would act like "gasoline poured on a fire." When it appeared that Five Sigma would not back off, war broke out. Buffett announced the B share offering. "Berkshire intends to provide a direct, low-cost means of investment in Berkshire so superior to the investments offered by the unit trust promoters that their products will be rendered unmarketable," the prospectus for the shares read.[196]

To discourage brokers from hyping the new stock, Berkshire arranged the offering through Salomon. The commission was purposely set low, giving little incentive to brokers to push investors into the initial public offering. Buffett also said the company would issue as many shares as the public wanted, thus minimizing the first-week price spike caused by a limited supply and a high demand.

On the front page of the prospectus, Buffett repeated Munger's message to Five Sigma: "Management does not believe that the company's stock is undervalued."[197]

At the 1996 annual meeting, a shareholder asked about Berkshire's shares being overvalued. Buffett replied that he had not said the shares were overvalued. He said they were "not undervalued." There's a distinction, Buffett insisted, obviously rankled that the subtlety had been missed by journalists and investors alike.

The distinction seemed fuzzy to many in the investment world. "There are a lot of questions legitimately as to why he's doing this," said, Derek Sasveld, a consultant at Ibbotson Associates Inc., a Chicago stock research and consulting firm. "It doesn't seem to be a completely logical situation."[198]

William LeFevre, senior market analyst at Ehrenkrantz King Nussbaum Inc. in New York, suspected Buffett's territory had been invaded. "His credibility is as high as it gets, and he doesn't want somebody making a buck off the name of Warren Buffett."[199]

Others, however, saw the structure of the vehicle, rather than the intrinsic value of the stock, as the source of Buffett's problem. At the 1996 annual meeting, Buffett described the unit trusts as "a high-commission product with substantial annual fees."

"Mr. Buffett has always been a champion of shareholder rights, and he doesn't like the fact that to buy into the unit investment trusts is not as economically feasible as buying the common stock," said James Mulvey, an analyst at Dresdner Securities USA Inc.[200]

With the Baby Bs, as investors called them, the same deal could be had with only the payment of a broker's commission.

*Barron's* columnist Alan Abelson dismissed the "not undervalued" statement—plus prospectus disclaimers that the company's intrinsic value could continue to grow at past rates—as mere pandering to regulators. "To Warren Buffett we say, truth wounds, cynicism kills—think on what ye have wrought and repent! There's still time to revise that prospectus. A small phrase—'just kidding!'—inserted on the front page right below those caveats will do the trick."[201]

Others, however, thought Buffett might have been understating the overvaluation problem. Stock market columnist Malcolm Berko ran a brief analysis of Berkshire for his readers, describing it as a closed-end mutual fund. Berko estimated that Berkshire (both A and B) was selling at a massive premium over its net asset value (NAV). Berko estimated the NAV of Berkshire A shares at $15,000. "So, in my opinion, you gotta be dumber than a bag of ball-peen hammers to pay a $21,000 premium over NAV to own BRKA," Berko wrote.[202]

This debate over the value of Berkshire's share price had an impact on the stock. The A shares quickly receded from a high of $38,000 back to the $33,000 range. The B shares were issued at $1,110. There was a price hop shortly after the offering, but the shares settled in at just over $1,000 within a few weeks.

The Berkshire B stock sold like ice in Arizona despite Buffett's frank—though somewhat perplexing—disclosure as to the intrinsic value of Berkshire Hathaway. At first, the company said it would issue 100,000 shares, but that number was increased four times. Ultimately, more than 517,500 were issued, doubling Berkshire's shareholder base to 80,000 individuals.

Buffett has used the money collected from the B shares to help build a more powerful company, and certainly one with more assets. However, as he always warned, size does not guarantee high performance. In fact, it may slow growth. Since 1996, certain ratios have been erratic, and Buffett has had some bad years. But it's not all bad news. For 2006, Berkshire's per-share book value of both A and B shares increased 18.4 percent. Over the 42 years Buffett has controlled Berkshire, its book value has grown an average of 21.4 percent compounded annually each year:

> *"We believe that [the 2006 gain in net worth of] $16.9 billion is a record for a one-year gain in net worth—more than has ever been booked by* any *American business, leaving aside boosts that have occurred because of mergers (e.g., AOL's purchase of Time Warner). Of course, Exxon Mobil and other companies earn far more than Berkshire; but their earnings largely go to dividends and/or repurchases, rather than building net worth."*[203]

## ADMIT YOUR MISTAKES

Buffett confesses to dozens of investment errors, including buying Berkshire Hathaway, a New England textile mill. The sagging textile business was finally closed down, but the corporate structure and name was retained as an investment vehicle. Investor Irving Kahn, who has known Buffett since his student days, observed, "Even a man with Warren's talents slips."[204]

Buffett takes his lumps with good humor:

*"Of course, some of you probably wonder why we are now buying Capital Cities at $172.50 per share given that this author, in a characteristic burst of brilliance, sold Berkshire's holdings in the same company at $43 per share in 1978–80. Anticipating your question, I spent a lot of time working on a snappy answer that would reconcile these acts.*

*"A little more time, please."*[205]

~

*"I've repressed my memory of the earlier sale of Cap Cities stock."*[206]

Buffett occasionally gives bum advice:

*"My only role with the* Washington Post's *sale of cellular phone properties was to recommend against the original purchase of the properties at one-fifth the price they sold for. And that's the last time they asked me.*

*They didn't pay attention to me the first time and they didn't ask the second time.*"[207]

It was a coup when, in 1998, Buffett acquired the vast and venerable reinsurance company Gen Re for $22 billion. The deal had two benefits: Not only was Buffett dancing within his circle of competence (in this case, insurance), but he also was in step with his more recent goal of expanding into global markets. Connecticut-based General Re holds a 78 percent stake in the world's oldest reinsurance company, Cologne Re, which does business in nearly 150 countries. Together, Gen Re and Cologne Re are both the oldest and the world's third-largest reinsurance operation.

Almost immediately after the purchase, Buffett discovered problems involving both underwriting and reserving that took years to correct. But that wasn't all. Buffett also had to wrestle with a Securities and Exchange Commission investigation into charges that some policies were knowingly written to falsely inflate client earnings. Worst of all, he had to go to the mat with Gen Re's derivative segment. The company, he admitted, was a problem child.

*"Unfortunately it was a 400-pound child, and its negative impact on our overall performance was large."*[208]

~

*"Long ago, Mark Twain said: 'A man who tries to carry a cat home by its tail will learn a lesson that can be learned in no other way.' If Twain were around now, he might try winding u a derivatives business. After a few days, he would opt for cats."*[209]

Years before buying Gen Re, Buffett had warned that derivatives were a sea where dragons lurk. General Re came equipped with a derivatives operation holding 23,218 contracts, one of them having a duration of a century. It took six years to shrink the number of derivatives to 2,890, and it cost Berkshire $404 million to get that far out of the business. Yet there were more losses to come.

Buffett spent 12 paragraphs of the 2005 annual report explaining General Re's derivative drama, saying he had cost shareholders a lot of money by not being decisive enough:

*"Both Charlie and I knew at the time of the Gen Re purchase that it was a problem and told its management that we wanted to exit the business. It was my responsibility to make that happen. Rather than address the situation head on, however, I wasted several years while we attempted to sell the operation . . . fault me for dithering. (Charlie would call it thumb sucking.)"*[210]

Nevertheless, Gen Re is a whopping, powerful insurance force; and both Warren and Charlie say they are pleased to own it. The company holds the highest possible marks from A. M. Best, Moody's, and Standard & Poor's. One of Berkshire's most valuable assets is insurance float (one shareholder call it "leverage in drag"), which Buffet can invest for insurance group profits. Gen Re provides nearly half of Berkshire's $49 billion float. Finally, in 2006, Buffett told shareholders they would no longer have to hear him bemoan General Re's derivatives. The portfolio had been reduced to an amount that was almost negligible and that posed no threat to the company.

## NO THUMB SUCKING

Charlie Munger has little tolerance for dawdling, or "thumb sucking." If you find a good company at a good price, why vacillate?

Such was the case back in 1972 when Buffett, Munger, and an early investing partner, Rick Guerin, bought See's Candy. Munger and Guerin found the opportunity in Los Angeles and called Buffett to suggest purchasing it. Buffett was at first reluctant; then the phone call got cut off. Within minutes, Buffett called back and gave the deal the green light. He'd checked the numbers; did a quick analysis; and, despite the fact the company was selling at $25 million (three times book value), found that it was a quality company with earning power and growth potential.

Over the years, Berkshire's stash of cash, along with Buffett's and Munger's quick brains, has allowed flash decisions:

> *"If I got a call this afternoon and somebody offered me A, B or—securities, assets or a business—and it looked like a good idea, we could sign a deal tonight. We move fast, and we always have cash."*[211]

And yet, Buffett sometimes is guilty of thumb sucking:

> *"My biggest lost opportunity was probably Freddie Mac (the mortgage-purchasing organization). We owned a savings and loan, and that entitled us to buy 1 percent of Freddie Mac stock when it first came out. We should have bought 100 S&Ls and loaded up on Freddie Mac. What was I doing? I was sucking my thumb."*[212]

## JOIN AA (AIRLINES ANONYMOUS)

In 1995, Buffett took a $268.5 million write-off for 75 percent of his $385 million investment in USAir. The shares' 9.25 percent dividend had not been paid since September 1994. In the spring of 1996, Buffett was searching for a buyer for the convertible preferred stock:

> *"That was a senior security. It was a mistake, but it wasn't a common equity we picked as a wonderful*

*business. There aren't that many wonderful businesses in the world."*[213]

Buffett explained in a speech in North Carolina why airlines are not an investor's friend:

*"The interesting thing, of course, is that if you go back to the time—and we're in the right state for that—from Kitty Hawk, net, the airline transport business in the United States has made no money. Just think if you'd been down there at Kitty Hawk and you'd seen this guy go up, and all of a sudden this vision hits you that tens of millions of people would be doing this all over the world someday. It would bring us all closer together and everything. You'd think, my god, this is something to be in on. Despite putting in billions and billions and billions of dollars, the net return to owners for the entire airline industry, if you'd owned it all, and you'd put up all this money, is less than zero. If there had been a capitalist down there, the guy should have shot down Wilbur. One small step for mankind and one huge step back for capitalism."*[214]

Buffett attributes his USAir purchase to temporary insanity. How will he fend off a future attack?

*"So now I have this 800 number; and if I ever have the urge to buy an airline stock, I dial this number and I say my name is Warren and I'm an airoholic. Then this guy talks me down on the other end."*[215]

Buffett may be in Airlines Anonymous, but he still struggles with his affection for flight-related businesses. His investment in USAir did not go well. Then he bought a corporate jet that, in a spasm of guilt, he named "The Indefensible." Later, after the Salomon Brothers crisis, he renamed it "The Defensible." His love affair with that jet ended in 1998 when he discovered a new object of aviation affection, NetJets.

> *"I'm not flying "The Defensible"—the very defensible. It didn't make sense for me to own 100 percent of a plane. I thought that was my only option when I did it. To pay for four or five times the capacity you need doesn't make any sense. Somebody who has a whole airplane is like a navy with one type of boat. They don't need one destroyer; they need a whole array. I'm on a different mission all the time. I'll have a 300-mile flight in the States, [or] a 1,200 mile trip, or I'll be flying over here (Europe) and I have 11 aircraft types or something to choose from."*[216]

NetJets sells fractional ownership of an aircraft, which allows people to buy a certain percentage of a specific airplane and use it or swap it for a proportional number of flight hours per year. It's so convenient that both Warren and Charlie (who used to fly commercial coach) use the service.

> *"Once you've flown NetJets, returning to commercial flights is like going back to holding hands."*[217]

Berkshire acquired the privately held company for $725 million in stock and cash. Alas, Buffett's sad aviation karma showed up again. NetJet's profitability slipped right away, mainly due to a shortage of appropriate equipment, to high operating costs (fuel), and to its involvement in European markets. NetJets lost (pretax) $10 million in 2004 and another $80 million in 2005. Buffett maintains hope that the company will turn a profit. In 2005, he wrote:

> *"Rich Santulli, one of the most dynamic managers I've ever met, will solve our revenue/expense problem. He won't do it, however, in a manner that impairs the quality of the NetJets experience. Both he and I are committed to a level of service, security, and safety that can't be matched by others."* [218]

Indeed, in 2006, the performance of NetJets improved, although it remained in the red. It was operating in the black in Europe, and Buffett reported that the value of the fleet was far greater than that of NetJets' three largest competitors.

Those involved in the airline industry often remind nervous flyers that the pilot's life is on the line right along with theirs, so he or she cares deeply about getting you safely on the ground. Buffett flies NetJets about 225 hours each year, and his family uses another 550 hours of flight time. So other clients—including Tiger Woods,

Kathie Lee Gifford, Calvin Klein, and the band N'Sync—can rest assured that they will get the same high-quality personnel and airplanes that the Buffetts do. It's a comforting thought.

## LEARN FROM YOUR MISTAKES

Buffett says he made one of his worst decisions at age 21 when he put 20 percent of his net worth in a gasoline station. Over the years, he figures, the error cost him about $800 million in lost economic opportunity.[219]

The first step to recovery is to stop doing the wrong thing:

> *"It's an old principle. You don't have to make it back the way you lost it."*[220]

Berkshire does not pay dividends to investors. They thus avoid double taxation and, with no effort on their part, continually reinvest their earnings. The exception was a 10-cent dividend Buffett paid to his partnership in 1967. Of that, he says:

> *"I must have been in the bathroom at the time."*[221]

NOTE: Buffett says that if the time comes when he believes shareholders can find more lucrative ways to invest than Berkshire can, he will pay a dividend.

The Salomon government bond scandal taught Buffett a lesson that he might have preferred to skip:

*"You won't believe this—because I don't look that dumb—but I volunteered for the job of interim chairman. It's not what I want to be doing, but it will be what I will be doing until it gets done properly.*[222]

A battalion of lawyers filing suits against Salomon helped focus Buffett's attention:

*"I may be the American Bar Association's Man of the Year before the year is over."*[223]

Buffett compared the year he spent in New York helping Salomon Brothers get back on its feet to war:

*"You do it because you have to, but you're not looking for another one."*[224]

Before the Salomon incident occurred, Buffett was asked why he made biting remarks about the banking industry, when Berkshire held a big stake in Salomon. Buffett replied:

*"Why are we vocal critics of the investment banking business when we have a $700 million investment in Salomon? I guess atonement is probably the answer."*[225]

## BUY STORYBOOK STOCKS

Buffett's favorite way of describing intrinsic value and margin of safety has literary qualities. His favorite companies, Buffett says, are like:

*"wonderful castles, surrounded by deep, dangerous moats, where the leader inside is an honest and decent person.*

*Preferably, the castle gets its strength from the genius inside; the moat is permanent and acts as a powerful deterrent to those considering an attack; and inside, the leader makes gold but doesn't keep it all for himself. Roughly translated, we like great companies with dominant positions, whose franchise is hard to duplicate and has tremendous staying power or some permanence to it.* "[226]

~

*"You need a moat in business to protect you from the guy who is going to come along and offer [your product] for a penny cheaper."*[227]

(For more on moats, see the sections "Appreciate Franchise Value" and "Respect Pricing Power," which follow in this chapter.)

Buffett performed a real-world analysis on his favorite storybook stock back in 1969:

*"When I buy a stock, I think of it in terms of buying a whole company, just as if I were buying the store down the street. If I were buying the store, I'd want to know all about it. I mean, look at what Walt Disney was worth on the stock market in the first half of 1966. The price per share was $53, and this didn't look especially cheap; but on that basis, you could buy the whole company for $80 million when* Snow

White, Swiss Family Robinson, *and some other cartoons, which had been written off the books, were worth that much [by themselves]; and then [in addition], you had Disneyland and Walt Disney, a genius, as a partner."*[228]

Following the 1996 merger of Cap Cities/ABC with Disney, Berkshire again held a strong position in Disney:

*"Owning* Snow White *(the movie) is like owning an oil field. You pump it out and sell it, and then it seeps back in again."*[229]

NOTE: Disney finds it can reissue *Snow White* every seven years.

And then there's Mickey Mouse:

*"The nice thing about the mouse is that he doesn't have an agent. You own the mouse. He's yours."*[230]

Nevertheless, Berkshire held the Disney shares for a while and then sold them. Disney, at the time, was experiencing management turmoil.

## SEEK EXCELLENT COMPANIES

*"You should invest in a business that even a fool can run, because someday a fool will."*[231]

~

*"In any business, there are going to be all kinds of factors that happen next week, next month, next year, and so forth. But the really important thing is to be in the right business. The classic case is Coca-Cola, which went public in 1919. They initially sold stock at $40 a share. The next year, it went down to $19. Sugar prices had changed pretty dramatically after World War I. So you would have lost half of your money one year later if you'd bought the stock when it first came public; but if you owned that share today—and had reinvested all of your dividends—it would be worth about $1.8 million. We have had depressions. We have had wars. Sugar prices have gone up and down. A million things have happened. How much more fruitful is it for us to think about whether the product is likely to sustain itself and its economics than to try to be questioning whether to jump in or out of the stock?"*[232]

~

*"Let's say you were going away for 10 years, and you wanted to make one investment, and you know everything you know now, and you couldn't change it while you're gone. What would you think about?*

*"I came up with anything in terms of certainty, where I knew the market was going to continue to grow, where I knew the leader was going to continue to be the leader—I mean worldwide—and where I knew there*

*would be big unit growth. I just don't know anything like Coke."*[233]

~

*"Charlie [Munger] made me focus on the merits of a great business with tremendously growing earning power, but only when you can be sure of it—not like Texas Instruments or Polaroid, where the earning power was hypothetical."*[234]

Buffett once explained to then General Foods president Philip Smith why he was buying the company's stock when nobody else was interested:

*"You've got strong brand names, you're selling three times earnings when other food companies are selling at six to seven times earnings, and you're loaded with cash. If you don't know what to do with it, someone else will."*[235]

In fact, General Foods was acquired by Philip Morris, which merged it into Kraft Food. Philip Morris is now known as Altria.

*"The definition of a great company is one that will be great for 25 or 30 years."*[236]

One reason for buying excellent companies (in addition to strong growth) is that once a purchase is made, the investor has only to sit back and trust the company's managers to do their jobs. In 1973, Buffett already owned a good-sized chunk of Berkshire, plus a bank in Illinois, an Omaha weekly newspaper, interest in a half dozen insurance companies, a trading stamp company, a chain of women's clothing stores, and a candy company. Yet he told a reporter, with no boastfulness:

*"I can almost do it with my hands in my pockets. I really live a pretty easy life."*[237]

~

*"I tell everybody who works for our company to do only two things to be successful. They are (1) think like an owner, and (2) tell us bad news right away. There is no reason to worry about the good news."*[238]

## STICK WITH QUALITY

*"It's far better to own a portion of the Hope diamond than 100 percent of a rhinestone."*[239]

~

From his boyhood, when he published a tipsheet called "Stableboy Selections," Buffett has shown an interest in horse racing:

*"There are speed handicappers and class handicappers. The speed handicapper says you try and figure out how fast the horse can run. A class handicapper says a*

*$10,000 horse will beat a $6,000 horse. Graham says, 'Buy any stock cheap enough, and it will work.' That was the speed handicapper. And other people said, 'Buy the best company, and it will work,' That's class handicapping."*[240]

NOTE: Buffett began as a speed handicapper but progressed to class handicapping.

## JUNK BONDS

When asked what he thought of junk bonds, Buffett replied:

*"I think they'll live up to their name."*[241]

Later asked why he bought $139 million of Washington Public Power Supply System (WPPSS, also known as WHOOPS) junk bonds in 1983 and 1984 when ratings indicated they were a high risk, Buffett answered:

*"We don't make judgments based on ratings. If we wanted Moody's and Standard & Poor's to run our money, we'd give it to them."*[242]

NOTE: The bonds, which did not default, offered a fixed 16.3 percent tax-free yield, resulting in a $22.7 million annual return.

Since then, Buffett has made money in the junk bonds of RJR Nabisco, Chrysler Financial, Texaco, Time Warner, and Amazon.com.

*"I'm not an engineer. I don't even know why the light goes on when I flip the switch. I do, however, know how to pick junk bonds."*[243]

In Berkshire's 2002 annual report, Buffett explained that investing in stocks and in junk bonds is similar in some ways:

*"Both activities require us to make a price-value calculation and also to scan hundreds of securities to find the very few that have attractive reward/risk ratios."*

Yet he has very different expectations from the two types of investments. While he expects all his stock purchases to reap profits, this is not the case with junk bonds:

*"Purchasing junk bonds, we are dealing with enterprises that are far more marginal. These businesses are usually overloaded with debt and often operating in industries characterized by low returns in capital. Additionally, the quality of management is sometimes questionable. Management may even have interests that are directly counter to those of debtholders. Therefore, we expect that we will have occasional large losses in junk issues. So far, however, we have done reasonably well in this field."*[244]

Charlie Munger explained that Berkshire owns many fixed-income and bond investments, both directly and through its insurance subsidiaries; and it doesn't bother him that Berkshire is investing in something called "junk."

"As long as Warren is doing it, I love to see it done," Munger said. "And we've made a few hundred million pretax dollars doing that over the years without much risk or fuss. So we have that extra category."[245]

## APPRECIATE FRANCHISE VALUE

Buffett describes franchise value as a moat around the castle of business. He uses Gillette as an illustration:

*"There are 20 to 21 billion razor blades used in the world a year. Thirty percent of those are Gillettes, but 60 percent by value are Gillettes. They have 90 percent market shares in some countries—in Scandinavia and Mexico. Now, when something has been around as long as shaving and you find a company that has both that kind of innovation, in terms of developing better razors all the time, plus the distribution power, and the position in people's minds. ... You know, here's something you do every day—I hope you do it every day—for $20 bucks [per year] you get a terrific shaving experience. Now men are not inclined to shift around when they get that kind of situation."[246]*

~

*"You go to bed feeling very comfortable just thinking about two and a half billion males with hair growing while you sleep. No one at Gillette has trouble sleeping."*[247]

NOTE: In 2004, Gillette was merged into Procter & Gamble, giving Berkshire a 3 percent ownership of P & G.

If you didn't grasp the concept of franchise value with Gillette, try it with Hershey bars:

*"If [you go into a store and] they say, 'I don't have Hershey bars, but I have this unmarked chocolate bar that the owner of the place recommends,' if you'll walk across the street to buy a Hershey bar or if you'll pay a nickel more for the [Hershey] bar than the unmarked bar or something like that, that's franchise value."*[248]

Or try the sweetheart test. There are times when a bargain price isn't the point:

*"You know this. They're not going to go home on Valentine's Day and say, 'Here, honey, here are two pounds of chocolates. I took the low bid.' It just doesn't work."*[249]

Coca-Cola has the strongest franchise value of any company on the planet:

*"If you run across one good idea for a business in your lifetime, you're lucky; and fundamentally, this (Coca-Cola) is the best large business in the world. It has got*

*the most powerful brand in the world. It sells for an extremely moderate price. It's universally liked—the per capita consumption goes up almost every year in almost every country. There is no other product like it.*[250]

The moat of franchise power offers strong protection:

*"A takeover [of Coca-Cola] would be like Pearl Harbor."*[251]

More than once, Buffett has acquired an interest in companies that faced serious financial difficulties, a condition that did not alter their franchise value:

*"It was similar to American Express in late 1963 when the salad oil scandal hit it. It did not hurt the franchise of the traveler's check or the credit card. It could have ruined the balance sheet of American Express, but the answer of course was that American Express with no net worth was worth a tremendous amount of money.*

*"And GEICO with no net worth was worth a tremendous amount of money, too, except it might get closed up the next day because it had no net worth; but I was satisfied that the net worth would be there. The truth is, a lot of insurance companies for the ownership of it would have put up the net worth. We would have put it up."*[252]

NOTE: In 1976, GEICO hit rough water after growing so fast; the company outpaced its capabilities. It recovered after Buffett bought in.

Buffett has lost interest in certain franchises. He once was one of RJR Nabisco's (owners of Reynolds Tobacco) largest shareholders, but he disposed of the shares in the early 1980s. Though he reportedly didn't object to Salomon Inc. making an RJR Nabisco investment in 1988, he declined to join. He is reported to have said:

> *"I'll tell you why I like the cigarette business. It costs a penny to make. Sell it for a dollar. It's addictive. And there's fantastic brand loyalty."* [253]

NOTE: Buffett later said he was quoting another person as having said this and meant the statement to be ironical. Nevertheless, there is sad truth in it.


## RESPECT PRICING POWER

A good business, Buffett explains, enjoys price flexibility. Pricing power is a kissing cousin to franchise value:

> *"If you own See's Candy, and you look in the mirror and say, 'Mirror, mirror on the wall, how much do I charge for candy this fall?' and it says, 'More,' that's a good business.* [254]

In 1986, Buffett anticipated the problems that would soon beleaguer the television industry due to its weakness in pricing power:

*"Essentially, TV had a lot of untapped pricing power many years ago, and they used it all up. They probably went a little beyond it. So the ability to price is not there to the same degree. I do not see galloping revenue gains beyond inflation in the network business; for years, they were getting it and they developed a way of life that was predicated upon it. And now, you're seeing an adjustment."*[255]

## FIND A COMPANY WITH CHEAP FLOAT (THEN TRY TO NOT MISPLACE THE COMPANY)

Buffett learned early that insurance company profits are based on superior investing of the premiums that accumulate awaiting the payment of a claim. This float, from all of Berkshire Hathaway's insurance businesses, is around $6.5 billion; and GEICO, which is now wholly owned by Berkshire, has produced $3 billion of it. The excess money does not belong to Berkshire Hathaway, but it can be used by it.

*"It has been a big mistake [by some securities analysts] to think of the value of the insurance operation as its book value alone, without regard to the value of the float."*[256]

Float exists in other businesses as well. Buffett observed:

*"Blue Chip Stamp used to be that kind of a business until it disappeared one day. Where was it? In the closet? I don't know."*

NOTE: Trading stamps were popular as a grocery shopping incentive in the 1950s and 1960s but lost ground to coupons and other gimmicks. However, before Blue Chip disappeared, Buffett had made considerable profit investing the float.[257]

## LEARN TO LIKE MONOPOLY

Freddie Mac (the Federal Home Loan Mortgage Corp.), a quasi-public corporation, provides a secondary market for home mortgages. Freddie Mac and its sister agency, Fannie Mae (Federal National Mortgage Assn.), control 90 percent of this business. The industry is a duopoly:

*"It's the next best thing to a monopoly."*[258]

~

*"Newspapers are a marvelous business. It's one of the few businesses that tend toward a natural, limited monopoly. Obviously, it competes with other advertising forms, but not with anything exactly like itself. Show me another business like that—there isn't one."*[259]

NOTE: Buffett made the preceding comment in 1986. Because of fundamental changes in demographics, retailing, and a proliferation of competing advertising possibilities such as the Internet, Buffett bumped newspapers down into a "good but not great" category and then lost interest entirely in new newspaper acquisitions.

During a circulation war between the *Buffalo Evening News* and the competing *Courier-Express*, the latter sued, accusing Buffett's newspaper of price fixing. A sore point was the rumor that Buffett had said owning a monopoly newspaper was like owning an unregulated toll bridge. When the comment came up in court, Buffett said:

> *"I have said in an inflationary world that a toll bridge would be a great thing to own if it was unregulated."*[260]

Why? asked the opposing attorney.

> *"Because you have laid out the capital costs. You build the bridge in old dollars, and you don't have to keep replacing it."*[261]

## FIND MANAGERS WHO THINK LIKE OWNERS

> *"I always picture myself as owning the whole place. And if management is following the same policy that I would follow if I owned the whole place, that's a management I like."*[262]

~

> *"The best CEOs love operating their companies and don't prefer going to Business Round Table meetings or playing golf at Augusta National."*[263]

Buffett often says that because he's not an expert in candy sales, encyclopedia publishing, or the uniform or shoe business (all of which Berkshire owns), he likes managers who are. Of H. H. Brown, shoe manufacturers and a major buyer of leather, Buffett says:

*"When a single steer topples, they know it."*[264]

## MANAGEMENT IS IMPORTANT, BUT A GOOD COMPANY IS MORE IMPORTANT

*"Our conclusion is that, with few exceptions, when management with a reputation for brilliance tackles a business with a reputation for poor fundamental economics, it is the reputation of the business that remains intact."*[265]

~

*"I like a business that, when it's not managed at all, still makes lots of money. That's my kind of business."*[266]

## AVOID THE INSTITUTIONAL IMPERATIVE (THE TENDENCY FOR CORPORATIONS TO ACT LIKE LEMMINGS)

*"Any business craving of the leader, however foolish, will be quickly supported by . . . studies prepared by his troops."*[267]

~

*"If you have mediocrity and you have a bunch of friends on the board, it's certainly not the kind of test*

*you put a football team through. If the coach of a football team puts 11 lousy guys out on the field, he loses his job. The board never loses their job because they've got a mediocre CEO. So, you've got none of that self-cleansing type of operation that works with all the other jobs."*[268]

## FAVOR COMPANIES THAT REPURCHASE THEIR OWN STOCK

When a company's own shares are trading at less than intrinsic value, Buffett says one of the best investments the company can make is to buy back its own shares. Does this mean he will acquire Berkshire shares if the price falls below intrinsic value?

*"That would make sense and I would do it, but only if Berkshire is cheaper than other stocks I'm interested in at the time."*[269]

## DON'T WORRY ABOUT DIVERSIFICATION

*"Diversification is a protection against ignorance. [It] makes very little sense for those who know what they're doing."*[270]

~

*"A lot of great fortunes in the world have been made by owning a single wonderful business. If you*

*understand the business, you don't need to own very
many of them.*"[271]

Buffett quotes Broadway impresario Billy Rose in
explaining the difficulties of overdiversification:

*"If you have a harem of 40 women, you never get to
know any of them very well."*[272]

## INVEST FOR THE LONG TERM

Buffett so deplores short-term trading that he has
suggested a 100 percent tax on profits made on stock
held for less than one year.[273]

*"Charlie and I expect to hold our stock for a very long
time. In fact, you may see us up here when [we're so
old that] neither of us knows who the other guy is."*[274]

~

*"We like to buy businesses. We don't like to sell, and we
expect the relationships to last a lifetime."*[275]

~

*"Most of our large stock positions are going to be held
for many years; and the scorecard on our investment
decisions will be provided by business results over that
period, and not by prices on any given day. Just as it
would be foolish to focus unduly on short-term prospects
when acquiring an entire company, we think it equally*

*unsound to become mesmerized by the prospective near-term earnings when purchasing small pieces of a company, i.e., marketable common stocks."*[276]

Not only does Buffett invest for the long haul, he hopes Berkshire Hathaway shareholders will keep their shares as long as possible:

*"If I had a club or if I [were] preaching at a church, I would not measure my success by how frequent the turnover of the congregation was or [what] the club membership would be. I would really like the idea that nobody wanted to leave their seats so that there wouldn't be a seat available for anybody else."*[277]

A corporate acquisition can be thought of this way:

*"It's a little like a romance for a while. You spend some time with them; and, you know, you have your first date. And then, finally, the big moment comes. The next day, do you want to start thinking about if somebody offers me 2X for this or 3X for this, would I sell it?"*[278]

Buffett says he's a "Rip Van Winkle" investor:

*"My favorite time frame for holding a stock is forever."*[279]

## TO SUM UP

*"Stocks are simple. All you do is buy shares in a great business for less than the business is intrinsically*

*worth, with managers of the highest integrity and ability. Then you own those shares forever."*[280]

Or, Buffett says, you can follow Will Rogers. Rogers said to study the markets carefully before buying a stock; then, "When the stock doubles, sell it." What if the stock doesn't double? "If it doesn't double, don't buy it."[281]

## AND WHEN YOU'VE BECOME WEALTHY BY FOLLOWING IN THE FOOTSTEPS OF BUFFETT, PAY YOUR DUES TO SOCIETY

One of the qualities that makes Buffett, his friends, and his colleagues unique is their attitude regarding their responsibility to others with whom they share the earth.

## INVESTING IS ONE WAY OF CONTRIBUTING TO THE PUBLIC WELL-BEING

*"Large gains in real capital, invested in modern production facilities, are required to produce large gains in economic well-being. Great labor availability, great consumer wants, and great government promises will lead to nothing but great frustration without continuous creation and employment of expensive new capital assets throughout industry. That's an equation understood by Russians as well as Rockefellers. And it's one that has been applied with stunning success in West*

*Germany and Japan. High capital-accumulation rates have enabled those countries to achieve gains in living standards at rates far exceeding ours, even though we have enjoyed much the superior position in energy.*"[282]

~

Although some investors profit, leveraged buyouts aren't always good for society. For one thing, substituting debt for equity reduces a company's taxes, which finance social programs.

*"Now when you read about Boone Pickens and Jimmy Goldsmith and the crew, they talk about creating value for shareholders. They aren't creating value; they are transferring it from society to shareholders. That may be a good or bad thing, but it isn't creating value—it's not like Henry Ford developing the car or Ray Kroc figuring out how to deliver hamburgers better than anyone else. . . . In the last few years . . . one [company] after another has been transformed by people who have understood this game. That means that every citizen owes a touch more of what is needed to pay for all the goods and services that the government provides.*"[283]

## WHEN REWARDS ARE DISPROPORTIONATE

Other people make equally valuable contributions to the safety, health, happiness, and well-being of society; but they earn less than he does, Buffett says:

*"This society provides me with enormous rewards for what I bring to this society."*[284]

~

*"I personally think that society is responsible for a very significant percentage of what I've earned. If you stick me down in the middle of Bangladesh or Peru or someplace, you'll find out how much this talent is going to produce in the wrong kind of soil. I will be struggling 30 years later. I work in a market system that happens to reward what I do very well—disproportionately well. Mike Tyson, too. If you can knock a guy out in 10 seconds and earn $10 million for it, this world will pay a lot for that. If you can bat .360, the world will pay a lot for that. If you're a marvelous teacher, this world won't pay a lot for it. If you are a terrific nurse, this world will not pay a lot for it. Now, am I going to try to come up with some comparable worth system that somehow [re]distributes that? No, I don't think you can do that. But I do think that when you're treated enormously well by this market system, where, in effect, the market system showers the ability to buy goods and services on you because of some peculiar talent—maybe your adenoids are a certain way, so you can sing and everybody will pay you enormous sums to be on television or whatever— I think society has a big claim on that."*[285]

~

*"I don't have a problem with guilt about money. The way I see it is that my money represents an enormous number of claim checks on society. It's like I have these little pieces of paper that I can turn into consumption. If I wanted to, I could hire 10,000 people to do nothing but paint my picture every day for the rest of my life. And the GNP would go up. But the utility of the product would be zilch, and I would be keeping those 10,000 people from doing AIDS research, or teaching, or nursing. I don't do that, though. I don't use very many of those claim checks. There's nothing material I want very much. And I'm going to give virtually all of those claim checks to charity when my wife and I die."*[286]

Buffett offered another example of how "claim checks" work in a eulogy he wrote for Omaha real estate developer Peter Kiewit (Buffett admired Kiewit because he saved his claim checks, leaving much of his $200 million estate to charity):

*"In essence, one who spends less than he earns is accumulating 'claim checks' for future use. At some later date, he may reverse the procedure and consume more than he earns by cashing some of the accumulated claim checks. Or he may pass them on to others—either during his lifetime by gifts or upon his death by bequests.*

*"[William Randolph] Hearst, for example, used up many of his claim checks in building and maintaining San Simeon. Just as the pharaohs did when building pyramids, Hearst commanded massive amounts of labor and material away from other societal purposes in order to satisfy his personal consumption desires.*

*"An army of servants catering to his personal whims—such as the employee in San Luis Obispo who spent much of a lifetime hauling ice daily to the bears in the private zoo—was unavailable to produce other goods and services useful to society in general."*[287]

Buffett's friend Bill Gates says he expects to run Microsoft until 2008 and then promises to focus on how to give his fortune away. Buffett expects that Gates will return some claim check to society:

*"He will spend time, at some point, thinking about the impact his philanthropy can have. He is too imaginative to just do conventional gifts."*[288]

## PAY YOUR TAXES AND DON'T COMPLAIN

When explaining that Berkshire paid federal taxes of $390 million in 1993, Buffett said:

*"Charlie and I have absolutely no complaints about these taxes. We work in a market-based economy that rewards our efforts far more bountifully than it does*

> *the efforts of others whose output is of equal or greater benefit to society. Taxation should, and does, partially redress this inequity. But we remain extraordinarily well treated.*"[289]

Buffett has written that a 100 percent tax on profits from the sale of a security that is held for less than a year—applied to everyone, including institutional investors—would make the United States more competitive. By forcing investors to hold their shares longer, the industry would be more stable.

> *"We talk a lot about competing in a world economy against foreign decision makers who operate with a business horizon of decades. Why not try pushing our own horizon out at least a year?"*[290]

As often is the case, Munger's position is similar to Buffett's, except that it reflects his Republican leanings. Munger explains: "I like a certain amount of social intervention (taxes, laws, etc.) that takes some of the inequity out of capitalism, but I abhor any system that allows rewarding fakes." For example, Munger says he dislikes worker's compensation for job-related injuries and disabilities because it is difficult to sort out the bogus claims.[291]

Buffett objected to President George W. Bush's tax cuts, especially on inheritance taxes, which he called "tax cuts for the rich." Instead, he favored tax reductions for low- and middle-income citizens, who were more likely to spend the money on pressing and current needs and, therefore, stimulate the economy.

> *"I hear this Republican message that we're rich as hell and we're not going to take it anymore. That doesn't make a lot of sense to me. I'm paying taxes at a lower rate than my secretary ... and frankly I think that's crazy."*[292]

Buffett's essay critical of the Bush tax cuts ran in the *Washington Post* in May 2003. Two weeks later, the president's Assistant Secretary for Tax Policy at the U.S. Treasury delivered a speech defending the plan, adding, "This means that a certain Midwestern oracle, who, it must be noted, has played the tax code like a fiddle, is still safe retaining all his earnings."

Buffett surmised that he was that certain oracle. He returned a volley in his next letter to shareholders:

> *"Alas, my 'fiddle playing' will not get me to Carnegie Hall—or even to a high school recital. Berkshire, on your behalf and mine, will send the Treasury $3.3 billion for taxes on its 2003 income, a sum equal to 2.5 percent of the total income tax paid by* all *U.S. corporations in fiscal 2003."*[293]

Buffett explained that Berkshire has only about 1 percent of the U.S. stock market valuation, and yet it is among the top-10 corporate taxpayers. Naturally Buffett had to end with a joke:

> *"I do wish, however, that Ms. Olson would give me some credit for progress I've already made. In 1944, I filed my first 1040, reporting my income as a 13-year-old newspaper carrier. The return covered three pages. After I claimed the appropriate business deductions, such as $35 for a bicycle, my tax bill was $7. I sent my check to the Treasury and it—without comment—promptly cashed it. We lived in peace."*[294]

In 2006, Berkshire Hathaway paid $4.4 billion in federal income tax on a return that ran 9,386 pages:

> *"In the last fiscal year, the U.S. government spent $2.6 trillion, or $7 billion per day. Thus, for more than half of one day, Berkshire picked up the tab for all federal expenditures, ranging from Social Security and Medicare to the cost of our armed services. Had there been only 600 taxpayers like Berkshire, no one else in America would have needed to pay any federal income or payroll taxes."*[295]

~

> *"I think I am undertaxed, but I do not send along any voluntary payments."*[296]

Nevertheless, both Buffett and Bill Gates say they would be willing to carry a heavier tax burden for the good of the nation. Buffett said the current tax system needs to be more progressive. He pointed out that many soldiers fighting in Iraq pay higher percentages of their income in taxes than he does.

*"I frankly think it's very unfair."*[297]

## GIVE AS GENEROUSLY AS YOU RECEIVE

The World Cup was in progress when Buffett announced that he would give $31 billion to the Bill and Melinda Gates Foundation (BMG), raising the foundation's pot of gold to $60 billion. Despite Italian zeal for soccer and the fact that Italy was victorious, Buffett and Gates—the two richest men in the world—dominated the news. Italy and the whole world stood in awe of Buffett's ability and willingness to give so much to charity.

The pledge of 85 percent of his fortune to worthy causes (another $6 billion was directed to various Buffett family foundations) is the most munificent act of giving in U.S. history. It far outshines the legacy of the two foremost U.S. philanthropists: railroad baron Andrew Carnegie and oil magnate John D. Rockefeller. Measured in 2006 dollars, Carnegie's trust amounted to $4.1 billion and Rockefeller's to $7.6 billion. The *Christian Science Monitor* hailed the Buffett/Gates collaboration as the dawning of a new "golden age of philanthropy."

*Fortune* magazine editor at large Carol Loomis asked Buffett if it wasn't "somewhat ironic for the second-richest man in the world to be giving untold billions to the first-richest man"? Buffett said:

*"When you put it that way, it sounds pretty funny. But in truth, I'm giving it through him—and, importantly, Melinda as well—not to him."*[298]

For years, Buffett endured criticism that he was too tight-fisted with his money. He had so much but gave too little of it to those in need. In his earlier years, Buffett and his wife, Susie, had a foundation that did fund charitable work; but it never seemed enough.

Buffett wasn't ready then. He still was preoccupied with building and consolidating Berkshire's strength and power. Furthermore, Buffett never considered it his job to give his money away. Being better at earning money than spending it, he figured he would create the wealth, building a bigger pile to be spent later.

*"Someone who was compounding money at a high rate, I thought, was the better party to be taking care of the philanthropy that was to be done 20 years out, while the people compounding at a lower rate should logically take care of the current philanthropy."*[299]

Destiny interfered when Susie died, dashing Warren's plans to leave the foundation work in her care.

*"If I had died before Susie and she had begun to distribute our wealth, [the Buffett Foundation] would have scaled up to a much bigger size. I came to realize that there was a terrific foundation that was already scaled up and that could productively use my money now."*[300]

Buffett's decision to favor Gates over his own foundation was both original in concept and consistent with his business practices. He never starts new companies; he either invests in stock of existing ventures or buys successful companies outright. Buffett told the Gates:

*"I hope that the expansion of BMG's giving is one of depth rather than breadth. You have committed yourselves to a few extraordinarily important but underfunded issues, a policy that I believe offers the highest probability of your achieving goals of great consequence."*[301]

With so much money in play, the collaboration could be nothing short of spectacular. The Buffett contribution makes BMG nearly six times the size of the next-largest private U.S. charity, the Ford Foundation. BMG's budget and resources are superior to even those of the World Health Organization (WHO). If the Gates Foundation were a country, its assets would make the fifty-fifth-largest economy in the world, larger even than the oil kingdom of Kuwait.

In the first year alone, Buffett's contribution will increase BMG's annual giving by $1.5 billion. If Berkshire Hathaway shares continue to increase in value, the award amount could be millions higher.

"To manage a $60 billion foundation has never been tried," observed Joel J. Orosz, distinguished professor of philanthropic studies at Grand Valley State University in Grand Rapids, Michigan. "We've never had a foundation of this size and now, of course, influence."[302]

Bill and Melinda Gates said they were "awed" by Buffett's decision and looked forward to having him on the board. "Warren has not only an amazing intellect but also a strong sense of justice. Warren's wisdom will help us do a better job and make it more fun at the same time."[303]

Buffett has always said that he wanted the people who distributed his wealth to be daring:

> *"I want my trustees to swing from the trees on a few projects that do not have natural funding constituencies but that are important to society. I tell them that if they start giving half a million to this hospital and half a million to that college, I will come back and haunt them. But if they spend a ton of money on something that flops, God bless them."*[304]

The donation's possible shock to the culture will be softened by the fact that Buffett's contributions to the various foundations will be stretched over a 20-year span.

Although the potential for alleviating pain, suffering, loss, and deprivation in the world is astounding, the powerful Buffett/Gates partnership is controversial. The *Guardian* summarized some issues this way: "For many African health ministers, pitching their plans to the Gates Foundation has become a bigger priority than seeking aid from Western countries. Is such concentration of power a good thing? Will Mr. Gates and Mr. Buffett crowd out other efforts? Indeed, its size alarms those concerned about backdoor privatization of universal health care."

"Nobody questions Mr. Gates's—or Mr. Buffett's—motives," the *Guardian* continued. "But their largesse, some activists fear, could make other public efforts irrelevant. Scientific journals have pondered how the Gates Foundation backing one route over another could distort research priorities. Since private foundations lack public accountability about the way they make decisions and choose priorities, could they be detrimental to the public good? There is also concern that foundations undermine efforts to increase the state's role—although increased state role is not always a good thing."[305]

In its article, the *Guardian* acknowledged that governments don't always focus on the greater good and themselves can be erratic supporters of worthy causes. The controversy over government funding of stem cell research is an example of how slow and painful reaching public consensus can be. Also, government priorities can shift. The budget for the U.S. National Institutes of Health (NIH) grew during the late 1900s and the first few years of the twenty-first century. By 2006, federal funding was flat at around $28 billion annually. The *Wall Street Journal* reports that the Bush administration planned to reduce funding even more, the first NIH budget declines since the 1970s.

The *Guardian*'s blowback was mild, however, compared to that of a few conservative groups: "It's too bad that Buffett and his family choose to dabble in so many social 'causes,'" wrote the Capital Research Center. "Some of his money is going to charities that protect certain animal species; some goes to radical environmental groups that intimidate companies that won't protect certain tree species; and some goes to groups whose mission is to reduce the human species by 'protecting' women from the prospects of children and childbirth. It's too bad that Buffett is so rich that when he funnels even a small portion of his wealth to his family's hodge-podge of personal interests, he gives away billions of dollars to charities, both worthy and unworthy. Call it the shame and glory of philanthropy."[306]

## THOUGHTS ON CHARITABLE GIVING

When Buffett announced the additional funding of the Susan Thompson Buffett Foundation and the foundations of other family members, he offered some thoughts (but not directives) on how to best use the money:[307]

- Focus on a relatively few activities that can make an important difference.
- Concentrate on needs that would not be met without your assistance. Conversely, avoid making small gifts to a multitude of organizations that have other sources of funds and likely would go forward without your help.
- Consider working with your siblings on important projects.
- Pay attention to your home community, but favor a broader view.
- Judge projects by how they match your goals and their chances for success, not by the person who makes the request.
- Expect to make mistakes. Nothing will be accomplished if you always walk the safe path.

## WHAT DOES THE BILL AND MELINDA GATES FOUNDATION DO?

Warren Buffett's dramatic and unexpected partnership with the Gates family was an inspired move that is important for a host of reasons. First of all, Bill and Melinda already were gaining a reputation for reshaping the world through their giving programs.

By putting Buffett's money in their hands, it became clear where it will be spent. It won't go to the ballet, the symphony, or the opera. It won't go to a big business school that will put Buffett's name on a hall. The money will be spent on improving world health, education, and eradicating hunger; in other words, it's going to social causes. It will be spread around the entire globe, but especially to the Americas and third-world countries.

The Gates Foundation is guided by the simple belief that "every life has equal value." Bill Gates says that some of the foundation money will be used to help provide a first-class education for every American child. "Can that be done in our lifetime? I'll be optimistic and say, 'Absolutely.'"[308]

The foundation also targets the world's three most destructive disease: malaria, HIV/AIDS, and tuberculosis. "I think we dream in our lifetime about an AIDS vaccine," added Melinda Gates.[309]

"With the Warren Buffett money, we can deepen the effort," Melinda Gates said. "Instead of one country, we can work in five. [Warren's] money lets us expand the global health efforts."[310]

While the BMG is known for tackling large-scale problems, such as HIV/AIDS, vaccinations for third-world children, world hunger, and falling education standards in the United States, it's also a foundation with a heart for the smaller guy with immediate needs. BMG granted $500,000 to Save the Children for relief efforts following the devastating May 2006 Java earthquake. It is replacing libraries obliterated by Hurricane Katrina in the Gulf Coast. In its earlier years, BMG even built a new baseball field for a small Nebraska town where the kids had little to do except play ball.

Some results of BMG's earlier work are already documented. It is estimated that 1.7 million deaths have been prevented through the work of the Global Alliance for Vaccines and Immunization (GAVI), which was formed in 2000 with the foundation's help.[311]

While Gates gets his fair share of criticism for social engineering, most admire the effort. His philanthropy earned Microsoft the number-one spot in the Harris Interactive/*Wall Street Journal* survey to rank best and worst companies.

## WILL BUFFETT'S GIFT AFFECT THE COMPANY?

This distribution of his Berkshire shares to charity, Buffett said, will have virtually no effect on the share price.

> *"Anybody who knows me also knows how I feel about making Berkshire as good as it can be, and that goal is still going to be there. I wouldn't do anything differently because I'm not capable of doing things differently."*[312]

In the letter notifying them of additional funding for their trusts, Buffett assured his heirs that Berkshire Hathaway would continue to be a mighty machine:

> *"I regard Berkshire as an ideal asset to underpin the long-term well-being of a foundation."*[313]

Buffett's dominant shareholder position had always been a stabilizing force because he held so many shares and sold so few of them. Typically, the turnover ratio for Berkshire is only 15 percent a year, a very low ratio for a large-cap stock. Since Buffett structured the gifts to be distributed over 20 years, he will be releasing his grip on the company slowly enough for investors and Wall Street to adjust. And yet, even if all the donated shares are sold every year, the turnover ratio would jump to only 17 percent. Buffett also pointed out that with his and Susie's stock in play, the shares will gain greater liquidity, making Berkshire's true market value become more apparent.

## THE LAST WORD

Publishers, bookstore owners, investors, fans, and imitators have long awaited a book that Buffett himself would write. In 1973, Buffett began discussing the project with a coauthor—*Fortune* editor at large and writer Carol J. Loomis. In a 1989 letter to Loomis, he wrote:

> *"The big hang-up—aside from a normal heavy dose of procrastination—is that if I ever do a book, I want it to be useful. This means good ideas—and ideas that have not already been presented. My most important ideas are straight from Ben Graham, and he stated them far better than I ever could.*
>
> *"If the book is to be biographical, I believe I should wait a while. I am enough of an optimist to hope that the most interesting chapters are yet to come."*[314]

Even though Loomis continues to be a close friend of Buffett and the most authoritative voice on Berkshire Hathaway, as time passed, hope for a biography faded. In 1997, Buffett allowed Yeshiva University law professor Lawrence A. Cunningham to repackage and publish letters from the annual report. *The Essays of Warren Buffett: Lessons for Corporate America* (Cardoza Law Review, 1997) allows access to the message without digging through stacks of documents.

Then came a new development. Alice D. Schroeder, insurance analyst at Paine Webber, was allowed unprecedented access to Buffett and managers of Berkshire's companies for her 1999 report on the company. That report became a best seller of sorts. Not long afterward came the announcement that Schroeder would write a book on Buffett and have the same access to him. With the working title of *The Snowball: How Warren Buffett Collected Friends, Wisdom, and Wealth*, it is scheduled to be published in 2008. Buffett will not coauthor the book, and the fact that Schroeder is an analyst rather than a journalist or an author gives the impression that the book will be less personal and more business oriented. Nevertheless, Buffett followers look forward to the book.

## Berkshire's Book Value vs. the S&P 500

| | Annual Percentage Change | | |
|---|---|---|---|
| Year | In Per-Share Book Value of Berkshire (1) | In S&P 500 with Dividends Included (2) | Relative Results (1)–(2) |
| 1965 | 23.8% | 10.0% | 13.8% |
| 1966 | 20.3 | (11.7) | 32.0 |
| 1967 | 11.0 | 30.9 | (19.9) |
| 1968 | 19.0 | 11.0 | 8.0 |
| 1969 | 16.2 | (8.4) | 24.6 |
| 1970 | 12.0 | 3.9 | 8.1 |
| 1971 | 16.4 | 14.6 | 1.8 |
| 1972 | 21.7 | 18.9 | 2.8 |
| 1973 | 4.7 | (14.8) | 19.5 |
| 1974 | 5.5 | (26.4) | 31.9 |
| 1975 | 21.9 | 37.2 | (15.3) |
| 1976 | 59.3 | 23.6 | 35.7 |
| 1977 | 31.9 | (7.4) | 39.3 |
| 1978 | 24.0 | 6.4 | 17.6 |
| 1979 | 35.7 | 18.2 | 17.5 |
| 1980 | 19.3 | 32.3 | (13.0) |
| 1981 | 31.4 | (5.0) | 36.4 |
| 1982 | 40.0 | 21.4 | 18.6 |
| 1983 | 32.3 | 22.4 | 9.9 |
| 1984 | 13.6 | 6.1 | 7.5 |
| 1985 | 48.2 | 31.6 | 16.6 |
| 1986 | 26.1 | 18.6 | 7.5 |
| 1987 | 19.5 | 5.1 | 14.4 |
| 1988 | 20.1 | 16.6 | 3.5 |

*(continued)*

## Berkshire's Book Value vs. the S&P 500
### *(continued)*

| Year | Annual Percentage Change | | |
| | In Per-Share Book Value of Berkshire (1) | In S&P 500 with Dividends Included (2) | Relative Results (1)–(2) |
| --- | --- | --- | --- |
| 1989 | 44.4 | 31.7 | 12.7 |
| 1990 | 7.4 | (3.1) | 10.5 |
| 1991 | 39.6 | 30.5 | 9.1 |
| 1992 | 20.3 | 7.6 | 12.7 |
| 1993 | 14.3 | 10.1 | 4.2 |
| 1994 | 13.9 | 1.3 | 12.6 |
| 1995 | 43.1 | 37.6 | 5.5 |
| 1996 | 31.8 | 23.0 | 8.8 |
| 1997 | 34.1 | 33.4 | 0.7 |
| 1998 | 48.3 | 28.6 | 19.7 |
| 1999 | 0.5 | 21.0 | (20.5) |
| 2000 | 6.5 | (9.1) | 15.6 |
| 2001 | (6.2) | (11.9) | 5.7 |
| 2002 | 10.0 | (22.1) | 32.1 |
| 2003 | 21.0 | 28.7 | (7.7) |
| 2004 | 10.5 | 10.9 | (0.4) |
| 2005 | 6.4 | 4.9 | 1.5 |
| 2006 | 18.4 | 15.8 | 2.6 |
| Compounded Annual Gain: | | | |
| 1965–2006 | 21.4% | 10.4% | 11.0% |
| Overall Gain: | | | |
| 1964–2006 | 361,156% | 6,479% | |

## Berkshire Hathaway Share Price
### An Intermittent Glance at Share Price
### Progression, 1962–2007

| Year | Share Price |
|---|---|
| 1962 | $ 7.56 |
| 1965 | 12 |
| 1977 | 120 |
| 1981 | 500 |
| 1988 | 4,200 |
| 1989 | 8,550 |
| 1996 | 38,000 |
| 1998 | 80,000 |
| 2000 (top of Internet/tech bubble) | 40,800 |
| 2002 | 72,750 |
| 2007 | 108,000 |

Figures are either mid-year or year-end, but are representative of the price for that year.

# Time Line

## The Warren Buffett and Berkshire Hathaway Saga

**1869** – Sidney Buffett opened the Buffet & Sons grocery store in the Dundee neighborhood of Omaha, Nebraska. Three generations of Buffetts operated it until it closed in 1959. Both Warren Buffett and his partner, Charlie Munger, worked there as boys, although not at the same time. They didn't meet until they were adults.

**1888** – The Hathaway Manufacturing company was founded in New Bedford, Massachusetts, as a cotton milling operation. Hettie Green, the notorious Witch of Wall Street, served on the company's board. In 1955, Hathaway merged with Berkshire Fine Spinning Associates to become Berkshire Hathaway.

**1930** – Warren Edward Buffett is born on August 30 in Omaha to stockbroker Howard Buffett and his wife, Leila.

**1941** – Eleven-year-old Warren, in partnership with his sister Doris, bought his first stock, six shares of Cities Service preferred, at $38 per share. Buffett sold at $40, and later the stock advanced to $200 per share.

**1943** – Warren told a friend that he would be a millionaire by age 30 or jump off the tallest building in Omaha.

**1945** – Warren devised an elaborate newspaper delivery route that earned about $175 a month. At 14, he invested $1,200 in 40 acres of Nebraska farmland.

**1947** – As a high school senior, Buffett partnered with a friend to buy a pinball machine that they placed in a barbershop. The business expanded to three machines and was later sold for $1,200.

**1949** – Buffett left the University of Pennsylvania Wharton School of Business to enroll at the University of Nebraska, Lincoln.

**1950** – After completing college in three years and increasing his savings to $9,800, Buffett applied to Harvard Business School. He was rejected and enrolled at Columbia instead, where he studied under investment legends Benjamin Graham and David Dodd.

**1951** – After learning that his professor, Ben Graham, was on the GEICO board, Buffett traveled to GEICO headquarters and, by tenacity, got a private lesson on the insurance business from the future president of the company.

**1951** – After earning his MBS at Columbia, Buffett applied to Ben Graham for a job at his investment firm. Graham suggested that it was not a good time to enter the business and turned him down. Buffett returned to Omaha to work in his father's firm. Warren bought a Texaco gasoline station, an investment that didn't work out. He also took a Dale Carnegie public speaking course and taught a night class in investments at the University of Nebraska.

**1952** – Warren and Susan Thompson, daughter of a local college professor, were married. Susie had been Warren's sister's roommate at Northwestern University.

**1954** – Warren kept in close touch with Ben Graham. Graham had a change of heart and offered Buffett a job. Warren, Susie, and babies moved to New York.

**1956** – Graham retired and closed the Graham-Newman partnership. By now, Buffett had accumulated $140,000. He returned to Omaha, where he set up his own partnership with $100 of his own money and $105,000 from family and friends. Graham referred many of his former clients to Buffett.

**1959** – Buffett was introduced to fellow Omaha native Charles T. Munger. He and Munger soon became partners, and Charlie eventually became vice chairman of Berkshire.

**1962** – Buffett Partnerships began purchasing shares of Berkshire Hathaway. Berkshire had been a major player in textiles, but the industry was in decline. Berkshire was selling at around $8 per share, well below its net worth.

**1965** – Buffett took control of Berkshire and named Ken Chase as its new president.

**1967** – Berkshire paid its first and only dividend: 10 cents per share.

**1969** – Although 1968 was his most successful year, Buffett said he no longer could find suitable bargains. He closed the partnership and liquidated assets. Among the assets he paid out were shares of Berkshire. Soon afterward, he began transforming Berkshire into the holding company it now is.

**1970** – Buffett penned his first annual letter to shareholders.

**1970** – Buffett contacted Katharine Graham and told her that he was acquiring substantial shares in the *Washington Post* Company but that he was not a predatory buyer. It was the beginning of a long friendship.

**1977** – Susan Buffett moved to San Francisco to start a life of her own. The couple never divorced and often traveled and attended family events together. Susie also served on the board of Berkshire Hathaway until her death.

**1979** – Buffett's net worth reached $620 million; and for the first time, he was among the Forbes 400 richest Americans. He started investing in ABC, the television company that now is part of Disney.

**1988** – Buffett began buying Coca-Cola shares, which then became part of Berkshire's core holdings.

**1992** – Buffett spent most of the year in New York serving as chairman of Salomon Brothers. He faced the daunting task of resolving issues surrounding an illegal bond-trading incident and saving Salomon Brothers.

**1993** – Buffett was number one on *Forbes* magazine list of richest people in the world. Bill Gates was number two.

**1995** – Berkshire took a $258.5 million write-off for its investment in USAir.

**1996** – Buffett decided to issue Berkshire Hathaway B shares to discourage opportunists who intended to establish mutual funds for those who couldn't afford to pay $38,000 or more for a single A share. Berkshire Hathaway established a web site www.berkshirehathaway.com.

**1998** – Buffett collected 129.7 million ounces of silver, representing 30 percent of the world's above-ground inventory. He bought most of the silver futures contracts at $4.32 per ounce, their lowest price in 650 years. By 2007, the price of silver had tripled. Berkshire acquired the huge reinsurance company General Re.

**2000** – Berkshire Hathaway became a derided "low-tech" stock as investors hotly pursued high-tech and Internet companies. The overheated market that became known as the Great Bubble ended on March 10. The Nasdaq traded that day at its to-date high of 5,132. That same day, Berkshire traded at $40,800, its lowest price since mid-1997.

**2001** – The Berkshire Hathaway insurance unit lost $2.2 billion in underwriting as a result of the 9/11 terrorist attacks on the World Trade Center.

**2004** – Susan T. Buffett died of a stroke following treatment for mouth cancer. She left an estate of $2.6 billion, mostly in Berkshire shares.

**2005** – The Berkshire Hathaway insurance unit lost $2.5 billion as a result of hurricanes Katrina, Rita, and Wilma.

**2006** – Buffett donated most of his wealth to charity, 85 percent to the Bill and Melinda Gates Foundation and additional amounts to the foundations of his three children. The money will be dispersed over a 20-year period. This is the largest act of charitable giving in U.S. history. Berkshire Hathaway experienced a single-year net-worth growth of $16.9 billion, a record one-year gain for any U.S. company, not counting gains caused by mergers. On his birthday, he married long-time companion, Astrid Menks.

# Endnotes

## INTRODUCTION

1. "The New Establishment 50," *Vanity Fair*, October 1995, p. 280.
2. Ibid.
3. "In from the Cold," *The Economist*, May 23, 1992, p. 86.
4. Bill Gates, "What I Learned from Warren Buffett," *Harvard Business Review*, January/February 1996.
5. Bob Reilly, "The Richest Man in America," *USWest*, Autumn 1987, p. 2.

## ABOUT LIFE

1. L. J. Davis, "Buffett Takes Stock," *New York Times Magazine*, April 1, 1990, p. 16. (Modified later by Buffett letter to author.)
2. Bob Reilly, "The Richest Man in America," *USWest*, Autumn 1987, p. 2.
3. L. J. Davis, "Buffet Takes Stock," *New York Times Magazine*, April 1, 1990, p. 16.
4. Bob Reilly, "The Richest Man in America," *USWest*, Autumn 1987, p. 2.
5. Robert McMorris, "Unparsimonious Billionaire Puzzled by Warren Buffett," *Omaha World-Herald*, December 3, 1987, p. B1.

6. Linda Grant, "Striking Out at Wall Street," *U.S. News & World Report*, June 20, 1994, p. 58.

7. William D. Orr and Pamela Holloway-Eiche, *First Gentleman's Cookbook* (Lincoln, NE: William D. Orr, 1987), p. 178.

8. Ann Hughey, "Omaha's Plain Dealer," *Newsweek*, April 1, 1985, p. 56.

9. *Forbes 400*, October 24, 1988, p. 155.

10. *New York Times*, May 20, 1990, as reported in Andrew Kilpatrick, *Of Permanent Value: The Story of Waren Buffett* (Birmingham, AL: AKPE, 1994), p. 568.

11. Robert Dorr, "Investor Warren Buffett Views Making Money as 'Big Game,'" *Omaha World-Herald*, March 3, 1985, p. 1.

12. Andrew Kilpatrick, *Of Permanent Value: The Story of Warren Buffett* (Birmingham, AL: AKPE, 1994), p. 81.

13. David C. Churbuck, "Games Grown-ups Play," *Forbes*, December 19, 1994, p. 308.

14. Bill Gates, *The Road Ahead* (New York: Viking Press, 1995), pp. 207–208.

15. Video prepared for and played at the Berkshire Hathaway annual meeting, 1996.

16. "Billionaires," *Forbes 400*, October 18, 1993, p. 112.

17. Berkshire Hathaway annual meeting, 1995.

18. L. J. Davis, "Buffett Takes Stock," *New York Times Magazine*, April 1, 1990, p. 16.

19. Warren Buffett, 1986 Capital Cities/ABC management conference.

20. Warren Buffett, "Oil Discovered in Hell," *Investment Decisions*, May 1985, p. 22.

21. Alan Gersten, "Buffett Faces Shareholders," *Omaha World-Herald*, May 21, 1986, p. 27.

22. Berkshire Hathaway annual meeting, 1991.

23. Sue Baggarly interview with Warren Buffett, WOWT-TV, Channel 6, Omaha, October 14, 1993.

24. Jim Rasmussen, "Billionaire Talks Strategy with Students," *Omaha World-Herald*, January 2, 1994, p. 17S.

25. Warren Buffett, Berkshire Hathaway annual meeting, 2000.

26. Berkshire Hathaway annual meeting, 1995.

27. Berkshire Hathaway annual meeting, 1991.

28. Carol J. Loomis, "The Inside Story of Warren Buffett," *Fortune*, April 11, 1988, p. 26.

29. Warren Buffett speech at Emory Business College, November 1989, as reported in Andrew Kilpatrick, *Of Permanent Value: The Story of Warren Buffett* (Birmingham, AL: AKPE, 1994).

30. Patricia E. Bauer, "The Convictions of a Long-Distance Investor," *Channels*, November 1986, p. 22.

31. *Forbes 400*, October 28, 1985, p. 118.

32. Bob Reilly, "The Richest Man in America," *USWest*, Autumn 1987, p. 2.

33. Patricia Bauer, "The Convictions of a Long-Distance Investor," *Channels*, November 1986, p. 22.

34. "The Oracle of Omaha Visits SBPM," *GW Business News*, 2003, www.gwu.edu/business.

35. Warren Buffett, Shaw Industries Convention, March 30, 2001.

36. John Rothchild, "How Smart Is Warren Buffett?" *Time*, April 3, 1995, p. 54.

37. Joshua Kennon, "Warren Buffett Timeline," *Investing for Beginners*, About.com.

38. Robert Dorr, "Buffetts Have Become 1st Billionaires in State," *Omaha World-Herald*, July 28, 1985, p. 1.

39. Alan Gersten, "Buffett Ranks 8th as 'Biggest Stakeholder,'" *Omaha World-Herald*, July 16, 1986, p. 29.

40. "Billionaires," *Forbes 400*, October 18, 1993, p. 112.

41. Art Buchwald, "The Burden of Being Second Best," *Los Angeles Times*, July 20, 1995, p. E4.

42. Roger Lowenstein, *Buffett: The Making of an American Capitalist* (New York: Random House, 1995), p. 111.

43. Mark M. Colodny, "Warren Buffett's Tuffest Critic," *Fortune*, June 3, 1991, p. 211.

44. Andrew Kilpatrick, *Of Permanent Value: The Story of Warren Buffett* (Birmingham, AL: AKPE, 1994), p. 237.

45. Kilpatrick, *Of Permanent Value*, p. 386.

46. Kathy McCormack, "Buffett's Crisis Control: Lay It Out as You See It," *San Diego Union*, September 3, 1992. (Modified later by Buffett letter to author.)

47. Liz Smith, "Lifestyles' Catches Elusive Billionaire," *New Jersey Star Ledger*, November 4, 1992.

48. "Warren Buffett Talks Business," PBS TV program produced by the University of North Carolina, Center for Public Television, Chapel Hill, 1995.

49. Ibid.

50. Warren Buffett, Berkshire Hathaway annual meeting, 2002.

51. Roger Lowenstein, *Buffett: The Making of an American Capitalist* (New York: Random House, 1995), p. 46.

52. Linda Grant, "Striking Out at Wall Street," *U.S. News & World Report*, June 20, 1994, p. 58.

53. John Train, *The Money Masters* (New York: Harper & Row, 1980), p. 5.

54. Brett Duval Fromson, "Are These the New Warren Buffetts?" *Fortune, 1990 Investor's Guide*, p. 98.

55. Bob Reilly, "The Richest Man in America," *USWest*, Autumn 1987, p. 2.

56. Jim Rasmussen, "Billionaire Talks Strategy with Students," *Omaha World-Herald*, January 2, 1994, p. 17S.

57. Beth Botts, et al., "The Corn-fed Capitalist," *Regardie's*, February 1986.

58. Interview with author, May 25, 1993.

59. Interview with Sue Baggarly, WOWT-TV, Omaha, October 14, 1993.

60. Berkshire Hathaway annual meeting, 1994.

61. Ron Suskind, "Legend Revisited: Warren Buffett's Aura as Folksy Sage Masks Tough, Polished Man," *Wall Street Journal*, November 8, 1991, p. 1.

62. Andrew Kilpatrick, *Of Permanent Value: The Story of Warren Buffett* (Birmingham, AL: AKPE, 1994), p. 65.

63. "Investor Buffett's Speculations Reap Artistic Returns," *Omaha World-Herald*, May 30, 1985, p. 1.

64. Berkshire Hathaway annual meeting, 1996.

65. Linda Grant, "The $4-Billion Regular Guy," *Los Angeles Times Magazine*, April 7, 1991, p. 36.

66. From a video made for and shown at the Berkshire Hathaway annual meeting, 1996.

67. Andrew Kilpatrick, *Of Permanent Value: The Story of Warren Buffett* (Birmingham, AL: AKPE, 1994), p. 72.

68. Warren Buffett speech, New York Society of Security Analysts, December 6, 1994.

69. Robert Lenzner, "Warren Buffett's Idea of Heaven: I don't have to work with people I don't like," *Forbes 400*, October 18, 1993, p. 112.

70. Robert McMorris, "Leila Buffett Basks in Value of Son's Life, Not Fortune," *Omaha World-Herald*, May 16, 1987, p. 17.

71. Patricia E. Bauer, "The Convictions of a Long-Distance Investor," *Channels*, November 1986, p. 22.

72. Bill Kaufman, "Meet Warren Buffett's Daddy," *The American Enterprise*, July/August 2003, p. 48.

73. Robert Lenzner, "Warren Buffett's Idea of Heaven: I don't have to work with people I don't like," *Forbes 400*, October 18, 1993, p. 40.

74. Robynn Tysver, "Warren Buffett Hits Campaign Trail," *San Diego Union-Tribune*, October 16, 1994, p. I-1.

75. *Chicago Tribune*, November 20, 2003, p. 1.

76. "The Money Men: How Omaha Beats Wall Street," *Forbes*, November 1, 1969, p. 82.

77. Warren Buffett, "What We Can Learn from Phil Fisher," *Forbes*, October 19, 1987, p. 40.

78. Alan Deutschman, "Bill Gates' Next Challenge," *Fortune*, December 28, 1992, p. 31.

79. Ibid.

80. Interview with author, Omaha, May 25, 1993.

81. SEC File No. HO-784, Blue Chip Stamps, et al./Warren Buffett, letter to Charles N. Huggins, December 13, 1972.

82. CNBC interview prior to Berkshire Hathaway annual meeting, 1999.

83. From a video prepared for and shown at the Berkshire Hathaway annual meeting, 1996.

84. Warren Buffett, "The 3 Percent Solution," *Washington Post*, September 14, 1993, p. A21.

85. *Forbes 400*, October 19, 1992, p. 93.

86. Berkshire Hathaway annual meeting, 1992.

87. John Huey, "The World's Best Brand," *Fortune*, May 31, 1993, p. 44.

88. Carol J. Loomis, "The Inside Story of Warren Buffett," *Fortune*, April 11, 1988, p. 26.

89. Berkshire Hathaway annual meeting, 1987.

90. Carol J. Loomis, "The Inside Story of Warren Buffett," *Fortune*, April 11, 1988, p. 26.

91. Robert Dorr, "Furniture Mart Handshake Deal," *Omaha World-Herald*, September 15, 1993, p. E1.

92. Beth Botts, et al., "The Corn-fed Capitalist," *Regardie's*, February 1986, p. 53.

93. Ibid., p. 45.

94. "Warren Buffett Talks Business," University of North Carolina, Center for Public Television, Chapel Hill, 1995.

95. Bernice Kanner, "Aw Shucks, It's Warren Buffett," *New York Magazine*, April 22, 1985, p. 52.

96. Michael Kelly, "Mrs. B. Cruises into Year 100," *Omaha World-Herald*, December 17, 1992, p. 17SF.

97. Linda Grant, "The $4-Billion Regular Guy," *Los Angeles Times Magazine*, April 7, 1991.

98. Bernice Kanner, "Aw Shucks, It's Warren Buffett," *New York Magazine*, April 22, 1985, p. 52.

99. John R. Hayes, "The Oversight Was Understandable," *Forbes*, April 26, 1993.

100. Andrew Kilpatrick, *Of Permanent Value: The Story of Warren Buffett* (Birmingham, AL: AKPE, 1994), p. 429.

## ABOUT FRIENDS

1. Bob Reilly, "The Richest Man in America," *USWest*, Autumn 1987, p. 2.

2. Ibid.

3. Adam Smith, *Supermoney* (New York: Random House, 1972), p. 198.

4. "Ah-nold teams up with Buffett," CNNMoney.com, August 13, 2003.

5. "The Oracle of Omaha visits SBPM," *GWBusiness News*, www.gwu.edu/business.

6. Carolyn Said, "Actor gets expert help on finance: Warren Buffett, 'Sage of Omaha,' is world's second-richest man, crackerjack investor," *San Francisco Chronicle*, August 14, 2003, www.sfgate.com.

7. Office of the Govenor, Arnold Schwarzenegger web site, "Workers' Compensation Reform," http://gov.ca.gov.

8. L. J. Davis, "Buffett Takes Stock," *New York Times Magazine*, April 1, 1990, p. 16.

9. Robert Dorr, "Ex-Omahan Traded Law for Board Room," *Omaha World-Herald*, August 31, 1977, p. B1.

10. Carol J. Loomis, "The Inside Story of Warren Buffett," *Fortune*, April 11, 1988, p. 26.

11. Robert Lenzner and David S. Fondiller, "The Not-So-Silent Partner," *Forbes*, January 22, 1996, p. 78.

12. Berkshire Hathaway annual meeting, 1996.

13. John Train, *The Midas Touch* (New York: Harper & Row, 1987), p. 70.

14. Andrew Kilpatrick, *Of Permanent Value: The Story of Warren Buffett* (Birmingham, AL: AKPE, 1994), p.489.

15. Robert Lenzner, "Warren Buffett's Idea of Heaven: I don't have to work with people I don't like," *Forbes 400* October 18, 1993.

16. Robert Lenzner and David S. Fondiller, "Meet Charlie Munger," *Forbes*, January 22, 1996, p. 78.

17. Brett Duval Fromson, "And Now, a Look at the Old One," *Fortune, 1990 Investor's Guide*, p. 98.

18. Robert Lenzner, "Warren Buffett's Idea of Heaven: I don't have to work with people I don't like," *Forbes 400*, October 18, 1993, p. 40.

19. Robert Dorr, "Buffett's Right-hand Man," *Omaha World-Herald*, August 10, 1986, p. 1.

20. Robert Lenzner and David S. Fondiller, "Meet Charlie Munger," *Forbes*, January 22, 1996, p. 78.

21. Berkshire Hathaway annual meeting, 1995.

22. Berkshire Hathaway annual meeting, 1996. (Modified later by Buffett letter to author.)

23. Roger Lowenstein, *Buffett: The Making of an American Capitalist* (New York: Random House, 1995), p. 75.

24. Robert Dorr, "Ex-Omahan Traded Law for Board Room," *Omaha World-Herald*, August 3, 1977, p. B1.
25. Carol J. Loomis, "The Inside Story of Warren Buffett," *Fortune*, April 11, 1988, p. 26.

## ABOUT FAMILY

1. Ron Suskind, "Legend Revisited: Warren Buffett's Aura as Folksy Sage Masks Tough, Polished Man," *Wall Street Journal*, November 8, 1991, p. 1.
2. Kim Winston, "Most Inspiring Person of the Year 2006—Warren Buffett," Beliefnet, www.beliefnet.com.
3. Robynn Tysver, "Warren Buffett Hits Campaign Trail," *San Diego Union-Tribune*, October 16, 1994, p. I-1.
4. "Exclusive: Buffett Kids React to Dad's Donation," *Good Morning America*, ABC News, June 29, 2006.
5. Robert Lenzner, "Warren Buffett's Idea of Heaven: I don't have to work with people I don't like," *Forbes 400*, October 18, 1993, p. 40.
6. "Warren Buffett Talks Business," University of North Carolina, Center for Public Television, Chapel Hill, 1995.
7. "Exclusive: Buffett Kids React to Dad's Donation," *Good Morning America*, ABC News, June 29, 2006.
8. Michael Kelly, "Susie Funny Like Her Dad," *Omaha World-Herald*, May 26, 1996, p. B1.
9. Berkshire Hathaway annual meeting, 1992.
10. *Outstanding Investor Digest*, March 6, 1989, p. 4.
11. Carol J. Loomis, "A Conversation with Warren Buffett," *Fortune*, June 25, 2006.
12. Jeff Bailey, "Buffett Children Emerge as a Force in Charity," *New York Times*, July 2, 2006.
13. Adam smith, "The Modest Billionaire," *Esquire*, October 1988, p. 103.
14. Michael Kelly, "Susie Funny Like Her Dad," *Omaha World-Herald*, May 26, 1996, p. B1.
15. Robert Dorr, "Investor Warren Buffett Views Making Money as Big Game,'" *Omaha World-Herald*, March 24, 1985, p. 1.

16. Linda Grant, "The $4-Billion Regular Guy," *Los Angeles Times*, Sunday, April 7, 1991, p. 36.
17. Letter to Susan A. Buffett from Warren E. Buffett, June 26, 2006, posted in various places on the Internet.
18. Pat Milton, "Buffett Gift to Help Improve Education," Associated Press, June 2006.
19. Cliff Kincaid, "The Media Adore Warren Buffett," Accuracy in Media, 2006, www.aim.org.media_monitor.
20. Jonathan McClellan and Robert Huberty, "Warren Buffett's Philanthropy," *Foundation Watch*, Capital Research Center, October 2006, p. 1.
21. "An-nold teams up with Buffett," CNNMoney.com, August 13, 2003.
22. Ron Suskind, "Legend Revisited: Warren Buffett's Aura as Folksy Sage Masks Tough, Polished Man." *Wall Street Journal*, November 8, 1991, p. 1.
23. *Outstanding Investor Digest*, March 6, 1989, p. 8.
24. *Outstanding Investor Digest*, June 23, 1989, p. 16.
25. John Train, *The New Money Masters* (New York: Harper & Row, 1989), p. 55.
26. Bill Gates, *The Road Ahead* (New York: Viking Press, 1995), pp. 240–241.
27. John Train, *The Midas Touch* (New York: Harper & Row, 1987), p. 2.
28. David Elsner, "It Works: Buying $1 for 40 cents," *Chicago Tribune*, December 8, 1985, p. 1.
29. Bernice Kanner, "Aw Shucks, It's Warren Buffett," *New York Magazine*, April 22, 1985, p. 52.
30. Carol J. Loomis, "The Inside Story of Warren Buffett," *Fortune*, April 11, 1988, p. 26.
31. Ron Suskind, "Legend Revisited: Warren Buffett's Aura as Folksy Sage Masks Tough, Polished Man," *Wall Street Journal*, November 8, 1991, p. 1.
32. Andrew Kilpatrick, *Of Permanent Value: The Story of Warren Buffett* (Birmingham, AL: AKPE, 1994), p. 40.
33. Ron Suskind, "Legend Revisited: Warren Buffett's Aura as Folksy Sage Masks Tough, Polished Man," *Wall Street Journal*, November 8, 1991, p. 1.
34. Ibid.

35. Robert Dorr, "Investor Warren Buffett Views Making Money as 'Big Game,'" *Omaha World-Herald*, March 24, 1985, p. 1.

36. Al Pagel, "Susie Sings for More than Her Supper," *Omaha World-Herald*, April 17, 1977.

37. Ibid.

38. Ibid.

39. Ibid.

40. Matt Schudel, "Susan T. Buffett, 72, Dies: Wife of Billionaire Investor," *Washington Post*, July 30, 2004, p. B6.

41. Beth Botts et al., "The Corn-fed Capitalist," *Regardie's*, February 1986, p. 45.

42. Ron Suskind, "Legend Revisited: Warren Buffett's Aura as Folksy Sage Masks Tough, Polished Man," *Wall Street Journal*, November 8, 1991, p. 1.

43. Jonathon McClellan and Robert Huberty, "Warren Buffett's Philanthropy," *Foundation Watch*, Capital Research Center, October 2006, p. 4.

44. Warren Buffett letter to the board of directors, Susan Thompson Buffett Foundation, June 26, 2006.

45. Robert McMorris, "Unparsimonius Billionaire Puzzled by Warren Buffett," *Omaha World-Herald*, December 3, 1987. (Modified later by Buffett letter to author.)

46. Robert McMorris, "Leila Buffett Basks in Value of Son's Life, Not Fortune," *Omaha World-Herald*, May 16, 1987, p. 17.

47. Sue Baggarly interview, WOWT-TV Omaha, October 14, 1993.

48. Robert McMorris, "Leila Buffett Basks in Value of Son's Life, Not Fortune," *Omaha World-Herald*, May 16, 1987, p. 17.

49. Ibid.

50. Ibid.

51. Linda Sandler, "Buffett's Savior Role Lands Him Deals Others Can't Get," *Wall Street Journal*, August 14, 1989, p. C1.

52. Robert McMorris, "Unparsimonious Billionaire Puzzled by Warren Buffett," *Omaha World-Herald*, December 3, 1987.

53. Ron Suskind, "Legend Revisited: Warren Buffett's Aura as Folksy Sage Masks Tough, Polished Man," *Wall Street Journal*, November 8, 1991, p. 1.

54. Michael Lewis, "The Temptation of St. Warren," *The New Republic*, February 17, 1992, p. 23.

# ABOUT WORK

1. Warren Buffett interview with author, Omaha, May 25, 1993.
2. Speech given by Warren Buffett at Columbia Graduate School of Business, October 27, 1993.
3. Bob Reilly, "The Richest Man in America," *USWest*, Autumn 1987, p. 2.
4. Roger Lowenstein, *Buffett: The Making of an American Capitalist* (New York: Random House, 1995), p. 20.
5. L. J. Davis, "Buffett Takes Stock," *New York Times Magazine*, April 1, 1990, p. 16.
6. Robynn Tysver, "Warren Buffett Hits Campaign Trail," *San Diego Union-Tribune*, October 16, 1994, p. I-1.
7. L. J. Davis, "Buffett Takes Stock," *New York Times Magazine*, April 1, 1990, p. 16.
8. Robert Dorr, "Investor Warren Buffett Views Making Money as 'Big Game,'" *Omaha World-Herald*, March 24, 1985.
9. "Eye," *Women's Wear Daily*, October 10, 1985, p. 10.
10. *Forbes 400*, October 22, 1990, p. 122.
11. Jonathan Liang, "Investor Who Piled Up $100 Million in the '60s Piles Up Firms Today," *Wall Street Journal*, March 31, 1977, p. 27.
12. Berkshire Hathaway annual meeting, 1988.
13. Linda Grant, "The $4-Billion Regular Guy," *Los Angeles Times Magazine*, April 7, 1991, p. 34.
14. "How Omaha Beats Wall Street," *Forbes*, November 1, 1969, p. 82. (Modified later by Buffett letter to author.)
15. Bernice Kanner, "Aw Shucks, It's Warren Buffett," *New York Magazine*, April 22, 1985, p. 52.
16. John Train, *The Midas Touch* (New York: Harper & Row, 1987), p. 5.
17. L. J. Davis, "Buffett Takes Stock," *New York Times Magazine*, April 1, 1990, p. 16.
18. "Expert on Investing Plans to Slow Down," *Omaha World-Herald*, February 25, 1968, p. 1. (Modified later by Buffett letter to author.)

19. Adam Smith, *Supermoney* (New York: Random House, 1972), p. 182.

20. David A. Vise and Steve Coll, "Buffett-watchers Follow Lead of Omaha's Long-term Stock Investor," *Washington Post*, October 2, 1987, p. D1.

21. "How to Live with a Billion," *Fortune*, September 11, 1989, p. 50.

22. L. J. Davis, "Buffett Takes Stock," *New York Times Magazine*, April 1, 1990, p. 16.

23. Jim Rasmussen, "Billionaire Talks Strategy with Students," *Omaha World-Herald*, January 2, 1994, p. 17S.

24. Ibid., p. 24.

25. "ABC Affiliates Hear Network's Fall Strategy," *Broadcasting*, June 9, 1986, p. 22.

26. "Warren Buffett Talks Business," University of North Carolina, Center for Public Television, Chapel Hill, 1995.

27. Larry van Dyne, "The Bottom Line on Katharine Graham," *The Washingtonian*, December 1985, p. 204.

28. Patricia E. Bauer, "The Convictions of a Long-Distance Investor," *Channels*, November 1986, p. 22.

29. Ibid., p. 24.

30. Berkshire Hathaway annual meeting, 1991.

31. Patricia E. Bauer, "The Convictions of a Long-Distance Investor," *Channels*, November 1986, p. 22.

32. Andrew Kilpatrick, *Of Permanent Value: The Story of Warren Buffett* (Birmingham, AL: AKPE, 2004), p. 367.

33. Ibid., p. 102.

34. Ann Hughey, "Omaha's Plain Dealer," *Newsweek*, April 1, 1985, p. 56.

35. Jim Rasmussen, "Brother, Can You Spare a Million?" *Omaha World-Herald*, October 10, 1993, p. 1A.

36. Associated Press, "Warren Buffett, Used Car Salesman?" February 13, 2007.

37. Berkshire Hathaway annual meeting, 1989.

38. Roger Lowenstein, *Buffett: The Making of an American Capitalist* (New York: Random House, 1995), p. 286.

39. *Forbes 400*, October 19, 1992, p. 93.

40. Robert Dorr, "Buffett Plans to Shut Down Finance Firm," *Omaha World-Herald*, June 2, 1969.

## ABOUT RUNNING A BUSINESS

1. "Buffett Report Makes *Times* List," *Omaha World-Herald*, April 22, 1985, p. B1.
2. "Warren Buffett Talks Business," University of North Carolina, Center for Public Television, Chapel Hill, 1995.
3. Ibid.
4. Gordon Matthews, "Wells' Stock Continues to Climb on Speculation Buffett Is Buying," *American Banker*, November 10, 1992, p. 16.
5. "Omahan Mum on His Ideas for Grinnell's Investments," *Omaha World-Herald,* July 18, 1980.
6. Salomon Inc.: A report by the chairman on the company's standing and outlook, *New York Times*, October 29, 1991.
7. Ibid.
8. Berkshire Hathaway annual meeting, 1991.
9. Ibid.
10. Berkshire Hathaway annual meeting, 1992.
11. Berkshire Hathaway annual meeting, 1991.
12. Alan Gersten, "Buffett Faces Shareholders," *Omaha World-Herald*, May 21, 1986, p. 27.
13. Berkshire Hathaway annual meeting, 1994.
14. Berkshire Hathaway annual meeting, 1991.
15. Robert Dorr, "Early Faith Made Many 'Buffett Millionaires,'" *Omaha World-Herald*, May 5, 1986, p. 1.
16. Judith H. Dobrzynski, "Warren's World," *Business Week*, May 10, 1993, p. 30.
17. Salomon Inc.: A report by the chairman on the company's standing and outlook, *New York Times*, October 29, 1991.
18. Patrick J. Reilley, "Closing Down Buffett's Buffet, *Foundation Watch*, Capital Research Center, January 2004, p. 4.
19. "Now Hear This,"*Fortune*, January 10, 1994, p. 20.

20. Salomon Brothers annual meeting, New York, May 1992.
21. Ibid.
22. Jeff Hull, "Insights on Warren Buffett—the Man, the Mogul, the Mentor, Video Ventures Inc., 2003.
23. John Train, *The Money Masters* (New York: Harper & Row, 1980), p. 23.
24. Ibid.
25. *Outstanding Investor Digest*, May 24, 1991.
26. Carol J. Loomis, "The Inside Story of Warren Buffett," *Fortune*, April 11, 1988, p. 26.
27. Warren Buffett, letters to shareholders, Berkshire Hathaway annual report, 2005, p. 79.
28. "Warren Buffett Talks Business," University of North Carolina, Center for Public Television, Chapel Hill, 1995.
29. Robert G. Hagstrom Jr., *The Warren Buffett Way* (New York: John Wiley & Sons, Inc., 1994), p. v.
30. Robert Lenzner, "Warren Buffett's Idea of Heaven: I don't have to work with people I don't like," *Forbes 400*, October 18, 1993, p. 40.
31. Carol J. Loomis, "The Inside Story of Warren Buffett," *Fortune*, April 11, 1988, p. 26.
32. en.thinkexist.com/quotes/alice_schroeder.
33. Warren Buffett, letter to Mr. and Mrs. William H. Gates III, June 26, 2006, widely circulated on the Internet.

# ABOUT INVESTING

1. Carol J. Loomis, "The Inside Story of Warren Buffett," *Fortune*, April 11, 1988, p. 26.
2. "The Forbes Four Hundred Billionaires," *Forbes 400*, October 27, 1986.
3. Warren Buffett, letter to shareholders, Berkshire Hathaway annual report, 2005, p. 20.
4. Warren Buffett speech, New York Society of Security Analysts, December 6, 1994.
5. Robert Lenzner, "Warren Buffett's Idea of Heaven: I don't have to work with people I don't like," *Forbes 400*, October 18, 1993, p. 40.

6. Berkshire Hathaway annual meeting, 1988.

7. Warren E. Buffett, "How Inflation Swindles the Investor," *Fortune*, May 5, 1977, p. 250.

8. Ibid.

9. "Warren Buffett Is in Stocks Anyway," *Fortune*, May 1977, p. 253.

10. Warren Buffett, "Investing in Equity Markets," quoted in Columbia University Business School, transcript of a seminar held March 13, 1985, p. 23.

11. Robert Dorr, "Investor Warren Buffett Views Making Money as 'Big Game,'" *Omaha World-Herald*, March 24, 1985.

12. Adam Smith, *Supermoney* (New York: Random House, 1972), p. 181.

13. L. J. Davis, "Buffett Takes Stock," *New York Times Magazine*, April 1, 1990, p. 16.

14. Warren Buffett correspondence to Benjamin Graham, July 17, 1970.

15. Warren Buffett speech, New York Society of Security Analysts, December 6, 1994.

16. Ibid.

17. Buffett interview with the author, Omaha, May 25, 1993.

18. Berkshire Hathaway annual meeting, 1992.

19. Warren Buffett speech, New York Society of Security Analysts, December 6, 1994.

20. Berkshire Hathaway annual meeting, 1995.

21. Warren Buffett speech, New York Society of Security Analysis, December 6, 1994.

22. Benjamin Graham, *The Intelligent Investor* (New York: Harper & Row, 1973), p. 216.

23. Benjamin Graham and David Dodd, *Security Analysis* (New York: McGraw-Hill, 1940), p. 43.

24. Benjamin Graham, "Current Problems in Security Analysis," transcripts of lectures, September 1946–February 1947, New York Institute of Finance, p. 102.

25. Robert Lenzner, "Warren Buffett's Idea of Heaven: I don't have to work with people I don't Like," *Forbes 400*, October 18, 1993, p. 40.

26. Anthony Bianco, "Why Warren Buffett Is Breaking His Own Rules," *Business Week*, April 15, 1985, p. 134.

27. William Ruane, interview with the author, June 1993.

28. Warren Buffett speech, New York Society of Security Analysts, December 6, 1994.

29. Ibid.

30. Patricia E. Bauer, "The Convictions of a Long-Distance Investor," *Channels*, November 1986, p. 22.

31. Warren Buffett interview with the author, Omaha, May 25, 1993.

32. Warren Buffett interview with the author, May 25, 1993, and interview with Charles Brandes, May 1993.

33. Terence P. Pare, "Yes, You Can Beat the Market," *Fortune*, April 3, 1995, p. 69. (Modified later by Buffett letter to author.)

34. L. J. Davis, "Buffett Takes Stock," *New York Times Magazine*, April 1, 1990, p. 16.

35. Linda Grant, "The $4-Billion Regular Guy," *Los Angeles Times Magazine*, April 7, 1991, p. 36.

36. Berkshire Hathaway annual meeting, 1996.

37. Ibid.

38. Leah Nathans Spiro and David Greising, "Why Amex Wooed Warren Buffett," *Business Week*, August 19, 1991, p. 97.

39. "Look at All Those Beautiful, Scantily Clad Girls Out There!" *Forbes*, November 1, 1974.

40. Anthony Simpson, *The Midas Touch* (New York: Dutton, 1990), p. 79.

41. Warren Buffett, letter to shareholders, Berkshire Hathaway annual report, 2001.

42. Warren Buffett, letter to shareholders, Berkshire Hathaway annual report, 2005, p. 20.

43. "Look at All Those Beautiful, Scantily Clad Girls Out There!" *Forbes*, November 1, 1974.

44. Patricia E. Bauer, "The Convictions of a Long-Distance Investor," *Channels*, November 1986, p. 22.

45. *Forbes 400*, October 1, 1985, p. 82.

46. Berkshire Hathaway annual meeting, 1994.

47. Ibid.

48. "Face Behind the Figures," *Forbes*, January 4, 1988.

49. Comment by Warren Buffett, Berkshire Hathaway annual meeting, 1992 (as reported in Herb Ross, "How to Buffett against the Perils of Perots," *Westfield Leader*, August 6, 1992).

50. Robert Lenzner, "Warren Buffett's Idea of Heaven: I don't have to work with people I don't like," *Forbes 400*, October 18, 1993, p. 40.

51. L. J. Davis, "Buffett Takes Stock," *New York Times Magazine*, April 1, 1990, p. 16.

52. Warren Buffett, "You Pay a Very High Price in the Stock Market for a Cheery Consensus," *Forbes*, August 6, 1979, p. 25.

53. Robert Lenzner, "Warren Buffett's Idea of Heaven: I don't have to work with people I don't like," *Forbes 400*, October 18, 1993, p. 40.

54. L. J. Davis, "Buffett Takes Stock," *New York Times Magazine*, April 1, 1990, p. 16.

55. Warren Buffett, letter to shareholders, Berkshire Hathaway annual report, 2005, p. 75.

56. Linda Grant, "The $4-Billion Regular Guy," *Los Angeles Times Magazine*, April 7, 1991, p. 34.

57. *Forbes 400*, September 13, 1982, p. 116.

58. Warren Buffett, letter to shareholders, Berkshire Hathaway annual report, 2003, p. 5.

59. Buffett, letter to shareholders, Berkshire Hathaway annual report, 2003, p. 5.

60. Buffett, letter to shareholders, Berkshire Hathaway annual report, 2003, p. 6.

61. Warren Buffett, letter to partners, January 20, 1966.

62. Jim Rasmussen, "Hometown Deal Pleases Buffett," *Omaha World-Herald*, October 21, 1992, p. 16.

63. Berkshire Hathaway annual meeting, 1996.

64. Adam Smith, "The Modest Billionaire," *Esquire*, October 1988, p. 103.

65. Warren Buffett, *Nightly Business Report*, PBS, December 13, 1994.

66. David Elsner, "It Works: Buying $1 for 40 cents," *Chicago Tribune*, December 8, 1985, Section 7, p. 1.

67. Alan Gersten, "Buffett Faces Shareholders," *Omaha World-Herald*, May 21, 1986, p. 27.

68. Ann Hughey, "Omaha's Plain Dealer," *Newsweek*, April 1, 1985, p. 56.

69. Andrew Kilpatrick, *Of Permanent Value: The Story of Warren Buffett* (Birmingham, AL: AKPE, 1994), p. 568.
70. Warren Buffett, "What We Can Learn from Phil Fisher," *Forbes*, October 19, 1987, p. 40.
71. Terence P. Pare, "Yes, You Can Beat the Market," *Fortune*, April 3, 1995.
72. Warren Buffett letter, April 15, 1994. Shared by Walter Schloss.
73. Warren Buffett and Walter Schloss, discussion, New York Society of Security Analysts, December 6, 1994.
74. Andrew Kilpatrick, *Of Permanent Value: The Story of Warren Buffett* (Birmingham, AL: AKPE, 1994), p. 62.
75. Berkshire Hathaway annual meeting, 1995.
76. Maria Mallory, "Behemoth on a Tear," *Business Week*, October 3, 1994.
77. Warren E. Buffett, "How Inflation Swindles the Equity Investor," *Fortune*, May 5, 1977, p. 250.
78. Robert Lenzner, "The Secrets of Salomon," *Forbes*, November 23, 1992, p. 123.
79. Warren Buffett, "You Pay a Very High Price in the Stock Market for a Cheery Consensus," *Forbes*, August 6, 1979, p. 15.
80. Warren E. Buffett, "The Security I Like Best," *Commercial and Financial Chronicle*, December 6, 1951.
81. Jeff Hull, "Insights on Warren Buffett — the Man, the Mogul, the Mentor," Video Ventures, Inc., 2003.
82. Jim Rasmussen, "Buffett Talks Strategy with Students," *Omaha World-Herald*, January 2, 1994, p. 17S.
83. Rasmussen, p. 17S.
84. Ibid.
85. Warren Buffett, letter to shareholders, Berkshire Hathaway annual report, 1990.
86. Buffett, letter to shareholders, Berkshire Hathaway annual report, 2006, p. 8.
87. Buffett, letter to shareholders, Berkshire Hathaway annual report, 2005, p. 19.
88. Buffett, letter to Rep. John Dingell, D-MI, chairman of the House subcommittee on oversight and investigations, March 1982.

89. Ibid.
90. "Look at All Those Beautiful, Scantily Clad Girls Out There!" *Forbes*, November 1, 1974.
91. Brett Duval Fromson, "Are These the New Warren Buffetts?" *Fortune, 1990 Investor's Guide*, p. 81.
92. Adam Smith, "The Modest Billionaire," *Esquire*, October 1988, p. 103.
93. Warren Buffett, letter to John Dingell, chairman of the House of Representatives Subcommittee on Oversight and Investigations, March 1982.
94. Brett Duval Fromson, "Warm Tip from Warren Buffett: It's Time to Buy Freddie Macs," *Fortune*, December 19, 1988, p. 33.
95. Berkshire Hathaway annual meeting, 1993.
96. Linda Grant, "Striking Out at Wall Street," *U.S. News & World Report*, June 20, 1994, p. 58.
97. Robert Lenzner and David S. Fondiller, "Meet Charlie Munger," *Forbes*, January 22, 1996.
98. Warren E. Buffett, "How to Solve Our Trade Mess without Ruining Our Economy," *Washington Post*, May 3, 1987, p. B1.
99. Berkshire Hathaway annual meeting, 1996.
100. John C. Coffee Jr., Louis Lowenstein, and Susan Ackerman, eds., *Knights, Raiders, and Targets* (New York: Oxford University Press, 1988), pp. 11–27.
101. Tatiana Pouschine with Carolyn Torcellini, "Will the Real Warren Buffett Please Stand Up," *Forbes*, March 19, 1990, p. 92.
102. "Warren Buffett Talks Business," University of North Carolina, Center for Public Television, Chapel Hill, 1995.
103. "Warren Buffett's $2-Billion Song and Dance," *Fortune*, March 4, 1996.
104. Gary Strauss, "Buffett's a Buddy to Targeted Firms," *USA Today*, August 9, 1989.
105. Linda Grant, "Striking Out at Wall Street," *U.S. News & World Report*, June 20, 1994, p. 58.
106. Linda Grant, "The $4-Billion Regular Guy," *Los Angeles Times Magazine*, April 7, 1991.
107. Frequently quoted. The author heard the comment at the 1994 Berkshire Hathaway annual meeting in Omaha.

108. Warren E. Buffett, "How Inflation Swindles the Equity Investor," *Fortune*, May 5, 1977, p. 250.

109. Robert Dorr, "Investor Warren Buffett Views Making Money as 'Big Game,'" *Omaha World-Herald*, March 21, 1985, p. 1.

110. Warren Buffett, "Investing in Equity Markets," quoted in Columbia University Business School, transcript of a seminar held March 13, 1985, p. 19.

111. Linda Grant, "Striking Out at Wall Street," *U.S. News & World Report*, June 20, 1994, p. 58.

112. Adam Smith, "The Modest Billionaire," *Esquire*, October 1988, p. 103.

113. Linda Grant, "Striking Out at Wall Street," *U.S. News & World Report*, June 20, 1994, p. 58.

114. James Fogarty, "Buffett Questioned in IBM Suit," *Omaha World-Herald*, Jaunary 24, 1980, p. C1.

115. Warren Buffett, "Investing in Equity Markets," quoted in Columbia University Business School, transcript of a seminar held March 13, 1985, p. 23.

116. Linda Grant, "The $4-Billion Regular Guy," *Los Angeles Times Magazine*, April 7, 1991, p. 36.

117. Linda Grant, "Striking Out at Wall Street," *U.S. News & World Report*, June 20, 1994, p. 58.

118. David A. Vise and Steve Coll, "Buffett-Watchers Follow Lead of Omaha's Long-term Stock Investor," *Washington Post*, October 2, 1987, p. D1.

119. Warren Buffett, "Reforming Casino Society," *Financial World*, January 20, 1987, p. 138, reprinted from *Washington Post*.

120. Michael Lewis, "The Temptation of St. Warren," *The New Republic*, February 17, 1992, p. 22.

121. Robert Lenzner and Davis S. Fondiller, "The Not-So-Silent Partner," *Forbes*, January 22, 1996, p. 78.

122. "Warren Edward Buffett," *Forbes 400*, October 21, 1991, p. 151.

123. Berkshire Hathaway annual meeting, 1995.

124. Robert Dorr, "Buffett Quickly Unloaded First Three Stock Shares," *Omaha World-Herald*, December 5, 1968.

125. Warren Buffett, letter to shareholders, Berkshire Hathaway annual report, 2006, p. 17.

126. Berkshire Hathaway annual meeting, 1988.

127. "Warren Buffett Talks Business," University of North Carolina, Center for Public Television, Chapel Hill, 1995.

128. Reuters, "Arnold & Buffett's Loaded Elephant Gun," September 24, 2002.

129. Warren Buffett, commentary as to Berkshire's holding in PetroChina Company Limited, www.Berkshirehathaway.com.

130. Ibid.

131. "Look at All Those Beautiful, Scantily Clad Girls Out There!" *Forbes*, November 1, 1974.

132. Jim Rasmussen, "Billionaire Talks Strategy with Students," *Omaha World-Herald*, January 2, 1994, p. 17S.

133. Warren Buffett, "Investing in Equity Markets," quoted in Columbia University Business School, transcript of a seminar held March 13, 1985, pp. 28–29.

134. Robert Lenzner, "Warren Buffett's Idea of Heaven: I don't have to work with people I don't like," *Forbes 400*, October 18, 1993, p. 40.

135. Associated Press and *New York Times* News Services, "Buffett Buys Out the Rest of GEICO," *San Diego Union-Tribune*, August 26, 1995, p. C1.

136. "The Appeal of a Lousy Business," *Forbes*, March 19, 1990, p. 96.

137. Ibid.

138. Berkshire Hathaway annual meeting, 1995.

139. Charlie Munger, Wesco annual meeting, 2002.

140. *Bloomberg News*, October 21, 2002.

141. Berkshire Hathaway annual meeting, 1993.

142. Jim Rasmussen, "Billionaire Talks Strategy with Students," *Omaha World-Herald*, January 2, 1994, p. 17S.

143. Andrew Kilpatrick, *Of Permanent Value: The Story of Warren Buffett* (Birmingham, AL: AKPE, 2004), p. 1133.

144. "Warren Buffett Talks Business," University of North Carolina, Center for Public Television, Chapel Hill, 1995.

145. Bob Reilly, "The Richest Man in America," *USWest*, Autumn 1987, p. 2.

146. "How Omaha Beats Wall Street," *Forbes*, November 1, 1969, p. 82.

147. "Warren Buffett Talks Business," University of North Carolina, Center for Public Television, Chapel Hill, 1995.

148. Roger Lowenstein, *Buffett: The Making of an American Capitalist* (New York: Random House, 1995), p. 234.

149. Warren Buffett speech, New York Society of Security Analysts, December 6, 1996.

150. "Warren Buffett Talks Business," University of North Carolina, Center for Public Television, Chapel Hill, 1995.

151. Berkshire Hathaway annual meeting, 1991.

152. Robert Dorr, "Buffett's Ad Seeks Businesses to Purchase," *Omaha World-Herald*, November 18, 1986, p. C1.

153. "Warren Buffett Triples Profits," *New York Post*, May 14, 1994, p. D1.

154. Warren Buffett, Berkshire Hathaway annual meeting, 1992.

155. Mark Hulbert, "Be a Tiger, Not a Hen," *Forbes*, May 25, 1992, p. 298.

156. Berkshire Hathaway annual meeting, 1996.

157. Berkshire Hathaway annual meeting, 1984.

158. 'Warren Buffett Talks Business," University of North Carolina, Center for Public Television, Chapel Hill, 1995.

159. *Wall Street Journal*, September 30, 1987, p. 17.

160. Robert Dorr, "Buffett's Ad Seeks Businesses to Purchase," *Omaha World-Herald*, November 18, 1986.

161. Terence P. Pare, "Yes, You Can Beat the Market," *Fortune*, April 3, 1995.

162. Roger Lowenstein, *Buffett: The Making of an American Capitalist* (New York: Random House, 1995), p. 132.

163. Advertisement, *Wall Street Journal*, November 17, 1986, p. 16.

164. Berkshire Hathaway annual meeting, 1989.

165. Warren Buffett speech, New York Society of Security Analysts, December 6, 1994.

166. Berkshire Hathaway annual meeting, 1993.

167. Warren Buffett speech, New York Society of Security Analysts, December 6, 1994.

168. L. J. Davis, "Buffett Takes Stock," *New York Times Magazine*, April 1, 1990, p. 16.

169. Warren Buffett speech, New York Society of Security Analysts, December 6, 1994.

170. Carol J. Loomis, "The Inside Story of Warren Buffett," *Fortune*, April 11, 1988, p. 26.

171. Berkshire Hathaway annual meeting, 1991.

172. Berkshire Hathaway annual meeting, 1996.

173. Alan C. Greenberg, *Memos from the Chairman* (New York: Workman Publishing, 1996).

174. Patricia E. Bauer, "The Convictions of a Long-Distance Investor," *Channels*, November 1986, p. 22.

175. Ibid.

176. "Lights! Camera! Cash Flow!" *Fortune*, September 6, 1993, p. 11.

177. Alan Bersten, "Buffett Faces Shareholders," *Omaha World-Herald*, May 21, 1986, p. 27.

178. Berkshire Hathaway annual meeting, 1994.

179. Berkshire Hathaway annual meeting, 1996.

180. Warren Buffett, Harvard University speech, 1998. Cited on en. wikipedia.org.

181. Judith H. Dobrzynski, "Warren's World," *Business Week*, May 10, 1993, p. 30.

182. Robert Dorr, "Buffett Says Firm's Performance 'Is Certain to Decline,'" *Omaha World-Herald*, May 22, 1985, p. C1.

183. Gary Weiss and David Greising, "Proof! Wall Street's Sorcerers Lose Their Magic," *Business Week*, January 27, 1992, p. 74.

184. Claude Bejet, "Coke and Candy," *Forbes*, June 19, 1995, p. 152.

185. "The New Establishment 50," *Vanity Fair*, October 1995, p. 280.

186. Berkshire Hathaway annual meeting, 1996.

187. Ibid.

188. Ibid.

189. Ibid.

190. Warren Buffett speech, New York Society of Security Analysts, December 6, 1994.

191. L. J. Davis, "Buffett Takes Stock," *New York Times Magazine*, April 1, 1990, p. 16.

192. "Buffett Wins Berkshire Approval for Cheaper Stock, Urges Patience," *Los Angeles Times*, May 7, 1996, p. D3.

193. Ibid.
194. Ann Kates, "Berkshire Hathaway Joins NYSE," *USA Today*, November 8, 1988.
195. Frank Lalli, "Buffett's New Stock: Looks great . . . but is less filling," *Money*, April 1996, p. 94.
196. Reed Abelson, "Market Place," *New York Times*, May 8, 1996, p. D4.
197. Frank Lalli, "Buffett's New Stock: Looks great . . . but is less filling," *Money*, April, 1996, p. 94.
198. Walter Hamilton, "Investor's Corner," *Investors Business Daily*, February 23, 1996.
199. Ibid.
200. Ibid.
201. Alan Abelson, "Manchurian Capitalist," *Barron's*, April 22, 1996, p. 1.
202. Malcolm Berko, "If Buffett Won't Buy Shares, Why Should You?" *San Diego Business Journal*, July 15, 1996, p. 41.
203. Warren Buffett, letter to shareholders, Berkshire Hathaway annual report, 2006, p. 3.
204. Irving Kahn commentary, New York Society of Security Analysts, December 6, 1996.
205. Warren Buffett, "Oil Discovered in Hell," *Investment Decisions*, May 1985, p. 22.
206. Alan Gersten, "Buffett Tells Shareholders What He Seeks in Firms," *Omaha World-Herald*, May 21, 1986, p. D1.
207. Berkshire Hathaway annual meeting, 1987.
208. Warren Buffett, letter to shareholders, Berkshire Hathaway annual report, 2003, p. 11.
209. Buffett, letter to shareholders, Berkshire Hathaway annual report, 2005, p. 10.
210. Ibid., p. 11.
211. *Wall Street Journal*, August 2, 2002.
212. *Business Week*, July 5, 1999.
213. Warren Buffett speech, New York Society of Security Analysts, December 6, 1994.

214. "Warren Buffett Talks Business," University of North Carolina, Center for Public Television, Chapel Hill, 1995.

215. Ibid.

216. *Time* Online, September 28, 2002.

217. Warren Buffett, letter to shareholders, Berkshire Hathaway annual report, 2006, p. 13.

218. *Time* Online, September 28, 2002.

219. Berkshire Hathaway annual meeting, 1992.

220. Berkshire Hathaway annual meeting, 1994.

221. "Warren Edward Buffett," *Forbes 400*, October 21, 1991, p. 151.

222. *Institutional Investor*, September 1991, as quoted in Andrew Kilpatrick, *Of Permanent Value: The Story of Warren Buffett* (Birmingham, AL: APKE, 1994), p. 307.

223. Andrew Kilpatrick, *Of Permanent Value: The Story of Warren Buffett* (Birmingham, AL: AKPE, 1994), p. 310.

224. Linda Grant, "How Buffett Cleaned Up Salomon," *U.S. News & World Report*, June 20, 1994, p. 64.

225. Berkshire Hathaway annual meeting, 1991.

226. Berkshire Hathaway annual meeting, 1995.

227. "Warren Buffett Talks Business," University of North Carolina, Center for Public Television, Chapel Hill, 1995.

228. "How Omaha Beats Wall Street," *Forbes*, November 1, 1969, p. 88.

229. Berkshire Hathaway annual meeting, 1996.

230. Ibid.

231. Bill Gates, "What I Learned from Warren Buffett," *Harvard Business Review*, January/February 1996, p. 148.

232. Warren Buffett, Berkshire Hathaway annual meeting, 1992.

233. Melissa Turner, *The Atlanta Constitution*, as quoted in Andrew Kilpatrick, *Of Permanent Value: The Story of Warren Buffett* (Birmingham, AL: APKE, 1994), p. 198.

234. Robert Lenzner, "Warren Buffett's Idea of Heaven: I don't have to work with people I don't like," *Forbes 400*, October 18, 1993, p. 40.

235. Bernice Kanner, "Aw Shucks, It's Warren Buffett," *New York Magazine*, April 22, 1985, p. 52.

236. Berkshire Hathaway annual meeting, 1996.
237. Sam Thornton, "Warren Buffett, Omahan in Search of Social Challenges," *Lincoln* (Nebraska) *Journal and Star*, March 18, 1973, p. 6F.
238. Berkshire Hathaway annual meeting, 1995.
239. Berkshire Hathaway annual meeting, 1995.
240. L. J. Davis, "Buffett Takes Stock," *New York Times Magazine*, April 1, 1990.
241. Robert Dorr, "Buffett says Firm's Performance Is 'Certain to Decline,'" *Omaha World-Herald*, May 22, 1984.
242. Robert Dorr, "Buffett Acknowledges Risk Factor in His Purchase of WPPSS Bonds," *Omaha World-Herald*, April 15, 1985.
243. Warren Buffett, NetJets sales evening, Chicago, IL, November 14, 2001, as reported in Andrew Kilpatrick, *Of Permanent Value: The Story of Warren Buffett* (Birmingham, AL: AKPE, 2004), p. 749.
244. Warren Buffett, letter to shareholders, Berkshire Hathaway annual report, 2002.
245. Charles Munger, Wesco Financial annual meeting, Pasadena, CA, 2002.
246. "Warren Buffett Talks Business," University of North Carolina, Center for Public Television, Chapel Hill, 1995.
247. Ibid.
248. Ibid.
249. Ibid.
250. John Huey, "The World"s Best Brand," *Fortune*, May 31, 1993, p. 44.
251. "Now Hear This," *Fortune*, April 10, 1989, p. 21.
252. Warren Buffett, "Investing in Equity Markets," quoted in Columbia University Business School, transcript of a seminar held March 13, 1985, pp. 11–12.
253. Bryan Burrough and John Helyar, *Barbarians at the Gate* (New York: Harper & Row, 1990).
254. Jim Rasmussen, "Billionaire Talks Strategy with Students," *Omaha World-Herald*, January 2, 1994, p. 17S.
255. Patricia E. Bauer, "The Convictions of a Long-Distance Investor," *Channels*, November 1986, p. 22.

256. Berkshire Hathaway annual meeting, 1996.

257. Ibid.

258. Brett Duval Fromson, "Warm Tip from Warren Buffett: It's Time to Buy Freddie Macs," *Fortune*, December 19, 1988, p. 33.

259. Ibid.

260. *Courier-Express v. Evening News*, testimony of Warren Buffett, pp. 50–52.

261. Ibid.

262. Jim Rasmussen, "Billionaire Talks Strategy with Students," *Omaha World-Herald*, January 2, 1994, p. 17S.

263. *Fortune*, April 11, 1991.

264. Berkshire Hathaway annual meeting, 1992.

265. Robert Lenzner, "Warren Buffett's Idea of Heaven: I don't have to work with people I don't like," *Forbes 400*, October 18, 1993, p. 40.

266. Jim Rasmussen, "Billionaire Talks Strategy with Students," *Omaha World-Herald*, January 2, 1994, p. 17S.

267. Linda Grant, "The $4-Billion Regular Guy," *Los Angeles Times Magazine*, April 17, 1991, p. 36.

268. Robert Lenzner, "Warren Buffett's Idea of Heaven: I don't have to work with people I don't like," *Forbes 400*, October 18, 1993, p. 40.

269. A paraphrase of Warren Buffett's statement at the Berkshire Hathaway annual meeting, 1991.

270. Berkshire Hathaway annual meeting, 1996.

271. Warren Buffett speech, New York Society of Security Analysts, December 6, 1996.

272. Linda Grant, "The $4-Billion Regular Guy," *Los Angeles Times Magazine*, April 7, 1991, p. 36.

273. David A. Vise and Steve Coll, "Buffett-Watchers Follow Lead of Omaha's Long-term Stock Investor," *Washington Post*, October 2, 1987, p. D1.

274. Berkshire Hathaway annual meeting, 1996.

275. Alan Gersten, "Buffett Faces Shareholders," *Omaha World-Herald*, May 21, 1986, p. 27.

276. Robert Dorr, "Newspaper Holdings Kind to Omaha Investor Buffett," *Omaha World-Herald*, April 16, 1978, p. 6J.

277. "Warren Buffett Talks Business," University of North Carolina, Center for Public Television, Chapel Hill, 1995.

278. Jim Rasmussen, "Billionaire Talks Strategy with Students," *Omaha World-Herald*, January 2, 1994.

279. Linda Grant, "Striking Out at Wall Street," *U.S. News & World Report*, June 20, 1994, p. 58.

280. Andrew Kilpatrick, *Of Permanent Value: The Story of Warren Buffett* (Birmingham, AL: AKPE, 1994), p. 568, quoting from *Forbes*, August 6, 1990.

281. Robert McMorris, "Investor Buffett Tells Secret: Follow Will Rogers' Advice," *Omaha World-Herald*, May 31, 1985, p. B1.

282. Warren E. Buffett, "How Inflation Swindles the Equity Investor," *Fortune*, May 5, 1977, p. 250.

283. Warren Buffett, 1988 Capital Cities/ABC management conference.

284. Berkshire Hathaway annual meeting, 1996.

285. "Warren Buffett Talks Business," University of North Carolina, Center for Public Television, Chapel Hill, 1995. (Modified later by Buffett letter to author.)

286. "Warren Buffett—The Pragmatist," *Esquire*, June 1988, p. 159.

287. Warren E. Buffett, "Kiewit Legacy as Unusual as His Life," *Omaha World-Herald*, January 20, 1980, p. 1.

288. Walter Isaacson, "In Search of the Real Bill Gates," *Time*, January 13, 1997, p. 57.

289. Berkshire Hathaway annual report, 1994.

290. Warren Buffett, "Reforming Casino Society," *Financial World*, January 20, 1987, p. 139 (reprinted from *Washington Post*).

291. Berkshire Hathaway annual meeting, 1996.

292. Warren Buffett, Columbia University speech, September 27, 2000.

293. Warren Buffett, letter to shareholders, Berkshire Hathaway annual report, 2003.

294. Ibid.

295. Buffett, Berkshire Hathaway annual report, 2006, p. 19.

296. Buffett, Berkshire Hathaway annual meeting, 1998.

297. The Buffettblog.buffettspot.com, 2005.

298. Carol J. Loomis, "A Conversation with Warren Buffett," *Fortune*, June 25, 2006.

299. Ibid.

300. "Warren Buffett to Give about $3B to Susan Thompson Buffett Foundation, More than $30B to the Gates Foundation, *Abortion News*, June 28, 2006.

301. Warren Buffett, letter to Mr. and Mrs. William H. Gates III, June 26, 2006. Posted on the Internet.

302. Pat Milton, "Buffett Gift to Help Improve Education," Associated Press, June 2006.

303. Ibid.

304. *Financial Times*, May 17, 1999.

305. Zoe Corbyn, "Too Much of a Good Thing," *Guardian*, May 22, 2007.

306. Ibid.

307. Jonathan McClellan and Robert Huberty, "Warren Buffett's Philanthropy," *Foundation Watch*, Capital Research Center, October 2006, p. 2.

308. Warren Buffett, letters to Buffett children, posted on various Internet sites, June 26, 2006.

309. Carol J. Loomis, "The global force called the Gates Foundation," *Fortune*, June 25, 2006.

310. Dan Harris, "Buffett-Gates Team: Construction of a Charity Empire?" ABC News, June 26, 2006.

311. Marilyn, Chase, "Melinda Gate, Unbound," *Wall Street Journal*, December 11, 2006, p. B1.

312. Susan Okie, M.D., "Global Health—The Gates-Buffett Effect," *New England Journal of Medicine* 355, no. 11 (September 14, 2006), pp. 1084–1088.

313. Carol J. Loomis, "A Conversation with Warren Buffett," *Fortune*, June 25, 2006.

314. Warren Buffett, letter to the board of directors, Susan Thompson Buffett Foundation, June 26, 2006.

315. Warren Buffett, Letter to the author, October 23, 1989.

Permissions

# Permissions

Permission has been granted by the following organizations for quotes appearing in this book:

Adam Smith, for quotes taken from *Supermoney*.

The Associated Press

Warren Buffett

*Channels*

Excerpts from *Forbes Magazine*, reprinted by permission of *Forbes Magazine* © FORBES, Inc.

*Fortune Magazine*, © 1977, 1988, 1990, 1992 Time, Inc. All rights reserved.

*Investment Decisions*

*Of Permanent Value: The Story of Warren Buffett*, © 1994 by Andrew Kilpatrick, reprinted by permission of the author.